JAGUAR

—MkI and MkII—

The Complete Companion

JAGUAR

─MkI and MkII─
The Complete Companion

NIGEL THORLEY

BAY VIEW BOOKS

First published 1986 by Temple Press
Reprinted 1987

This edition published 1989 by
Bay View Books Ltd
13a Bridgeland Street
Bideford, Devon EX39 2QE
Reprinted 1990

Editor Charles Herridge

ISBN 1 870979 08 7
Printed in Hong Kong

Acknowledgments

There are many people I would like to thank for their help and guidance in the preparation of this book. In particular I would like to thank Jaguar Cars PLC. Compiling an historical reference book of this nature would not have been possible without access to the factory production records and I therefore must thank Alan Hodge for allowing me that facility. The very fact that Jaguar Cars have kept all production records dating back to the "SS" days is a clear example of the care and consideration they have always put into their products.

I would also like to especially thank friend, journalist and eminent Jaguar historian Paul Skilleter for his initial encouragement and subsequent advice.

It would be impossible to list all the other people who have helped in the preparation of this book. I will at least offer thanks to the libraries, garages, car owners, officials of the Jaguar Clubs and friends who gave their willing assistance.

Not least I ought to thank my wife Pauline for her understanding whilst burning the midnight oil and my editor Charles Herridge for having faith in my ability to write this work and patience whilst awaiting its completion.

I dedicate this book to them all.

Nigel Thorley

Contents

Introduction

As an avid supporter of the Jaguar marque and a particular enthusiast of the compact Mark I and II models, I was very pleased to be given the opportunity to write a book specifically about these cars.

The postwar compact saloons played an important role in the development and history of Jaquars Cars Limited. Well loved by everyone, these models pioneered monocoque construction and can safely be considered as the forerunners of all modern Jaguars. The compact saloons were not only great money-earners for the Company but brought prestige and success through their unrivalled competition history.

Within the context of their market, Mark Is and IIs were cheap to buy, economical to maintain and run, good looking, and faster than most other mass produced cars of the period. They could arguably be classed as the first true GT sports saloons. They were a total success and must be considered a tribute to the genius of Sir William Lyons and the workforce at Browns Lane.

In this publication I have attempted to cover the total concept of the compact saloons from the first 2.4 of 1956 to the final 240, and I have considered it vital to deal with the Daimler derivatives which were, after all, variants on the Mark II theme. For the purist I have tried to cover the many modifications in detail, and to avoid repetition from other publications I have not made use of contemporary roadtests. As far as the competition side is concerned, due to space limitation I have only been able to touch on this wide-ranging subject. For the general enthusiast I have discussed restoration and maintenance and attempted to offer some help to those interested in purchasing one of these cars. Coverage has also been given to some of the more unusual cars, and for the true fanatic mention is made of the toys and models based on the compact Jaguars.

Nearly all the information contained in these pages is based on historical fact. Not everything is known about the Mark Is and IIs and I doubt whether all will ever be revealed. Nevertheless I hope this book will prove of interest to enthusiasts of the series. I wish you all good reading.

Nigel Thorley

A Brief History of Jaguar

The general history of the Jaguar company and its cars has been covered in great detail many times before. Nevertheless, I feel it is only proper to refresh the reader's memory of the salient points of this great British company, the cars produced and the genius of their creator, Sir William Lyons.

William Lyons was born on the 4th September 1901. Little could anyone have realised the importance this man would play in the British motor car industry. After leaving school he spent a short time in the motor trade until he met William Walmsley (the son of a neighbour in King Edward Avenue, Blackpool) who manufactured motorcycle sidecars at the rear of the family home. Lyons spent much of his spare time with motorcycles and was very taken with the design of Walmsley's sidecar, so much so that he convinced him that they should join forces in a business venture manufacturing the sidecars on a full-time basis.

With help from his father William left his job in 1922 to commence business with Walmsley under the name of The Swallow Sidecar Company. The business operated from premises in Bloomfield Road, Blackpool, of quite a modest size. After a short time they needed more space and therefore took up the option on further premises at Back Woodfield Road, Blackpool, and later again in John Street, followed in 1926 by a complete move to Cocker Street.

Lyons had always been a fan of the Austin Seven motor car but had considered that the production body styling could be vastly improved upon. As the Austin was certainly one of the most popular small cars of its day, both Lyons and Walmsley could see the potential in developing the car further with a more stylish body. A rolling chassis was acquired and they set about designing their own body. The end result, unveiled in 1927, was smart and fashionable but still cheap and economical to run. The main advantage of the

Sir William Lyons, the genius behind Jaguar.

new body style lay in its individuality. The success of the Austin Swallow (as it was known) led to bodies being produced on other manufacturers' chassis including Alvis, Clyno, Fiat, Morris, Standard and Wolseley.

Production of sidecars and Swallow car bodies continued at an increasing rate and both partners realised that to get the skilled labour necessary for the future expansion of their business, it would be important to move nearer to the heart of the motor industry, the Midlands. The subsequent move, to Foleshill in Coventry to be exact, took place in 1928 and it was here that William Lyons formulated his ideas to produce his own motor-cars. He made arrangements with the Standard Motor Company for the supply of modified chassis and in 1931 the SS1 and SSII cars were born.

The SSI was a sleek, low two seater sports saloon with a six cylinder Standard engine. The car was particularly good looking, epitomising the fast, expensive sports car of the day but at a price substantially below anything else on offer from other manufacturers. "The £1000 look at the £300 price" was quoted – the SSI saw the start of the value for money theme continued to this day by Jaguar. The SSII was a smaller version based on a four cylinder Standard engine but employing a similar body style.

In the following year the SSI underwent a minor face lift with some slight modifications and the company went from strength to strength. William Walmsley left the business in 1934 to pursue his interest in caravans and in 1935 William Lyons introduced his SS90 and SS100 sports cars, true sports cars in their own right. The SS100 was to become Lyons' most memorable pre-war product. The same year also saw the introduction of the first four-door saloons, known as SS Jaguars , available initially in 1½ and 2½ litre Standard-engined versions and followed in 1938 by a 3½ litre model, all models again using Standard chassis. Lyons launched his new saloons at the Mayfair Hotel in London, encouraging the assembled press to guess the price of the new range, but no-one could estimate anywhere near the astonishingly low £395 set by Lyons – another example of Lyons' policy of offering the most for the least price. Part of his secret lay in the fact that the 1½ litre SS Jaguar was offered at a ridiculously low price to encourage volume sales, therefore bringing down the cost of parts used in the larger engined models.

During the war motor-car production ceased and the SS factory was turned over to helping the war effort. During this time, whilst fire-watching, Lyons, along with his engineers Heynes, Baily and Hassan, worked out plans for the manufacture of new engines for the post-war car range. After the war production recommenced initially with slightly updated models from the pre-war range until 1948 when the Mark V Saloon was announced. This was a redesign of the existing SS Jaguar saloon but employing a much wider body with extensive trim modifications and an entirely new independent front suspension; the Mark V was to become an interim model leading up to the release of the entirely new Mark VII saloon in 1950. (There never was a Mark VI due to a conflict of model numbers with Bentley.)

Returning for the moment to 1948, the star of the motor show was not the Mark V saloon but a brand new Jaguar sports car (the SS name having been totally dropped by this time), the XK120. This sleek, aluminium bodied two seater took the motoring world by storm. Perfectly proportioned and with a new, highly advanced, twin overhead camshaft straight six engine (the first Jaguar to utilise the 3.4 litre XK power unit) it could realistically reach a maximum speed of 120mph as its model number implied. It was also planned to run a smaller engined version known as the XK100 (utilising a four cylinder 2 litre version of the same power unit) but as orders for the XK120 were so overwhelming, the smaller engined car never went into production. The XK120 was originally intended as a short-term production project until the introduction of the big Mark VII saloon but it was soon realised that production would have to continue and even be stepped up to meet demand for the sports car. Over 12,000 XK120s were to be built between 1948 and 1954.

At the 1950 motor show the next new Jaguar model was to appear, the Mark VII saloon – the "prima ballerina" as it was known. This large luxury car had the same 3.4 litre power unit as the XK120 and was just as much an instant success. The flowing bodywork matched the styling of the XK120, and the car offered exceptional value for money at just under £1000. On its initial release in America over 500 orders were taken.

At the end of 1950 Jaguar Cars Limited moved yet again, this time to Browns Lane, Allesley in Coventry, site of one of the old war-time shadow factories. The early fifties were truly great years for Jaguar both in sales and in competition successes through their race developed models, the C types and later D Types winning the Le Mans 24 hour race in 1951, 1953, 1955, 1956 and 1957. 1954 saw the development of the XK120 into the XK140, leading in 1955 to the introduction of the first truly compact Jaguar saloon, the 2.4 litre, aimed at a wider market than the larger, by then modified, Mark VIIM.

Just after the release of the "new" compact Jaguar saloon William Lyons was knighted but in 1957 tragedy struck Jaguar when, on 12th February, a fire broke out in the factory, devastating production for a time. Despite this enormous blow to morale production recommenced within days, leading to the introduction of the larger engined (3.4 litres) compact saloon on the 26th February. Also in that year Jaguar introduced a further development of the XK sports car in the form of the XK150, followed closely by the latest model in the larger saloon car field, the Mark 1X (the last Jaguar to be produced with a separate chassis).

1959 brought with it the introduction of the Mark II revised versions of the compact saloons (now officially known as the Mark Is), this time offered with three engine choices, 2.4, 3.4, or 3.8 litres. In 1960 the Daimler Car Company was acquired and one year later the Guy commercial vehicle business. 1961 also saw the introduction of a new big Jaguar saloon, the Mark X, and yet another Jaguar model to take the world by storm, the fabulous E Type sports car, released in Geneva.

In 1963 Jaguar bought Coventry Climax, who made racing engines and fork-lift trucks. As the sixties progressed, so Jaguar introduced more and more models and engine configurations – the S Type saloon (based on the Mark II but with more comfort and an independently sprung rear end reminiscent of the E Type's), the 420 saloon (an S Type with modified front end treatment and a 4.2 litre version of the XK engine), and the 2.5 litre V8 Daimler engined model based on the Mark II Jaguar saloon shell.

In 1968 Sir William Lyons resigned as Managing Director (but stayed on as Chairman), handing over to F.R. (Lofty) England, the man who led Jaguar to success in the competition field. At this time Jaguar's model range consisted of the E Type sports car (now in Series II form), the 240 and 340 (latest models from the Mark II range), S Type saloons, 420 saloons and the massive 420G (developed from the original Mark X) plus the accompanying Daimler models. Later in that year Jaguar were to introduce their XJ6, which was ultimately to replace all other saloon car models. Initially in 2.8 and 4.2 litre versions (still using the XK power unit), the XJ6 has been the mainstay of Jaguar production right up to the present day. As if by foregone conclusion the XJ was voted "Car of the Year" in 1969. In the early seventies Jaguar introduced an entirely new engine, their magnificent twin camshaft V12 of 5.3 litres, which was inserted into the E Type and XJ shells. After production of the E Type ceased, Jaguar introduced the XJS grand touring car with the V12 engine and more recently with their latest engine development, the 3.6 litre slant-six AJ6 aluminium unit.

The Jaguar company is now going through a great revival with full order-books and an ever increasing share of the luxury car market both at home and abroad. With the introduction of the new AJ6 power unit, the imminent release of the XJ6 replacement (XJ40), and the probable introduction in the not too distant future of a new compact saloon (XJ80) and the F Type sports car, Jaguar are set to continue their success story.

A New Masterpiece

"To the already famous range of Jaguars exemplified by the Mark VII and the XK140 models, comes the 2.4 litre saloon, a brilliant newcomer in which will be found the embodiment of all the highly specialised technical knowledge and engineering achievement that have gained for the name of Jaguar the highest international repute."

The above was taken from the first brochure produced by Jaguar on the 2.4 litre compact saloon in 1956, and echoes the faith Jaguar had in their new car. The 2.4 was the forerunner of all modern Jaguars, embodying the technique of unitary construction, and gave rise to no less than four body shapes and thirteen distinct model titles housing a total of five different engine configurations.

To trace the development of the postwar Jaguar compact saloon we must look back to the early fifties, when William Lyons realised that there was a gap in his range of cars, between the sporting two seater XK and the opulent Mark VII luxury five seater, for a smaller sporting saloon which could carry four or five people in the utmost luxury and yet at the same time not lack in performance or economy. The new model was thus aimed at the motoring requirements of a much larger section of potential Jaguar customers. William Lyons also needed high volume production utilising many of the parts from his other cars in order to bring down component costs in the same way as he had before the war with the 1½ litre SS saloon.

The development of the new compact saloon took place over a period of three years with the help of the Pressed Steel Company, and over £100,000 was invested in the new model although the car was inevitably built to a selling price geared to hit the mass market. Perhaps ironically, the 2.4 litre proved to be the most expensive project undertaken by Jaguar up to that time because it broke entirely new ground for the company with its monocoque construction, new suspension, engine configuration, etc. It is interesting to record that, apparently, no one enjoyed the development work on the new car, but the end result was a truly magnificent, if somewhat over-engineered, vehicle.

It had initially been envisaged that the new saloon would employ the 2 litre four cylinder version of the XK power unit originally planned for the XK100 sports car back in 1948, this engine having a slight weight advantage over the six cylinder unit and obviously being of more compact dimensions, which made it ideally suited to a smaller saloon body. Although the four cylinder engine was responsive enough, the company thought the six cylinder version, with its inherent smooth running characteristics, was more suitable for a car of the quality associated with the Jaguar marque. The six cylinder engine was also more acceptable to the North American market, which was an important factor as William Lyons had high hopes for the new model abroad. Although the existing six cylinder XK engine was finally decided upon, it was to be in an entirely new configuration of 2.4 litres (2,483cc) brought about by reducing the stroke of the 3.4 litre engine to 76.5mm from 106mm but retaining the same bore of 83mm. The new engine revved faster, which made up for some of the loss of power. Carburation was by way of twin Solex downdraught carburettors (type B32-PB1-5/s) instead of the usual S.U. type to be found on other Jaguars; a manually operated choke mechanism was fitted, actuated by a lever situated on the dashboard. A long cylindrical air cleaner and silencer of AC manufacture were employed on an inverted T-shaped duct of rectangular design. This fitted over the intakes of the two

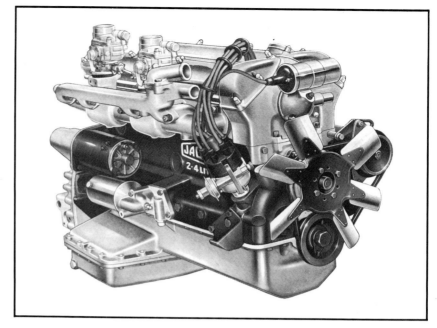

The six cylinder 2.4 litre XK engine. It had the same cylinder head as the 3.4 but the stroke was shorter and Solex carburettors replaced the SUs.

carburettors and the air was drawn in through a duct from a small dummy horn grille situated on the front of the nearside wing adjacent to the radiator grille. Unfortunately, this early type air intake trunking was straight through, allowing the accumulation of dirt unless regular attention to the filter was carried out. Later this trunking was modified and an oil bath air cleaner was introduced.

The new engine produced 112bhp at 5,750rpm and could return up to 28mpg in the compact body-shell of the 2.4. The 2.4 engine was some three inches less tall than the 3.4 litre version and somewhat lighter, contributing to economy. Interchangeability of parts was a major advantage of utilising the six cylinder engine, for despite the new capacity the cylinder heads were interchangeable between the two engine sizes and even the bearing sizes of the 2.4 were the same as in the XK140. Because of the reduction in stroke and the perhaps over-sized bearings, the 2.4 litre unit was immensely strong and had an exceptionally stiff crankshaft. The general balance of the engine was good and Jaguar engineers were well pleased with the end result.

Engine compartment of the 2.4.

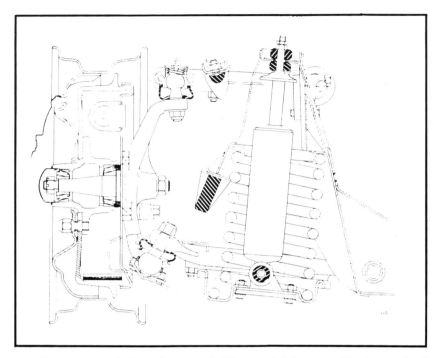

For the transmission of the new 2.4 litre model, Jaguar utilised a standard Moss gearbox with synchromesh on second, third and fourth gears as fitted to the Mark VII saloon, with power transmitted via a Borg and Beck 9″ dry plate clutch. Laycock de Normanville overdrive (on fourth gear only) was available on the Special Equipment models.

The front suspension on the new car was completely different to that of previous Jaguar saloons and used a separate front subframe of fabricated pressed steel to which were attached rear inclined wishbones of unequal length, stub axle carriers, coil springs and Girling telescopic dampers. The steering unit and idler assembly (of conventional Burman recirculating-ball type) was also bolted to this cross-member along with the track rod and tie-rods. The coil springs were housed in turrets at each end of the suspension cross-member and were retained at the lower end by seat pans bolted to the lower wishbones. Each coil spring was controlled by a telescopic direct-acting hydraulic damper mounted in the centre of the spring. The top of the damper was attached directly to the cross-member turret; the bottom bolted to a mounting bracket which in turn attached to the coil spring seat pan. The upper wishbone levers were mounted at the fulcrum shaft end on rubber and steel (Metalastic) mountings and the outer ends of the wishbone levers were bolted to the upper wishbone ball joint which in turn attached to the stub axle carrier. The inner ends of the lower wishbones were mounted on similar Metalastic bushes and the outer ends bolted to the lower ball joint which in turn attached to the stub axle carrier.

The front wheel hubs were supported on two tapered roller bearings, the inner races of which fitted on a shaft located in a tapered hole bored in the stub axle carrier. An anti-roll bar was fitted between the two lower wishbones, attached to the chassis side members by rubber insulated blocks.

The whole front suspension assembly was attached to the body underframe at four points using Metalastic blocks, enabling the bodyshell to be entirely insulated against road shocks and vibrations. The weight of the car being supported on these rubber blocks also gave side location of the front axle (fore and aft movement being controlled by the torque arms with rubber mountings).

Steering on the new model proved somewhat heavy and low geared, a characteristic of all subsequent versions of the Mark I and II models. The

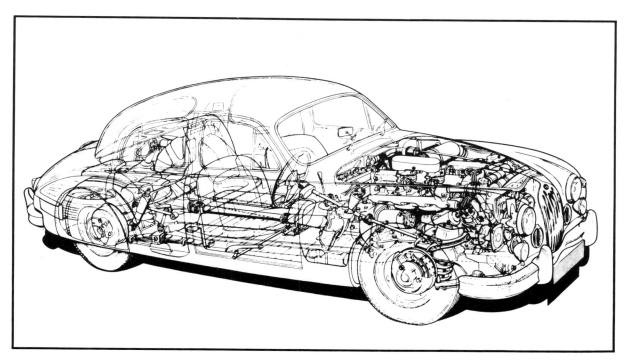

Cutaway showing detail of construction and mechanical aspects of the 2.4 saloon.

steering column was split by two rubber-mounted universal joints leading to a seventeen inch Bluemels steering wheel of the same design as fitted to other Jaguar cars of this period, adjustable for fore and aft movement by undoing a knurled ring on the column just behind the steering wheel. Many owners found that when the steering wheel was extended to its furthermost position the horn became inoperative (the horn being operated by a large push-button in the centre of the steering wheel).

For the rear suspension, long cantilevered springs (employing five leaves upside down) were used. The rear ends of the springs were attached to the axle via rubber bonded bushes and the springs encased in a specially designed block of rubber. The centres of the springs were carried within the box section members which ran from the front to the rear of the car. The front ends of the springs were mounted on simple rubber pads. The upward extension of the brackets on the axle carried two forward facing torque arms which reacted on the crossmember across the back of the rear seat area, again using rubber bushes. Side location of the live rear axle was via a Panhard rod and Girling telescopic dampers were used as at the front.

Rear suspension arrangement.

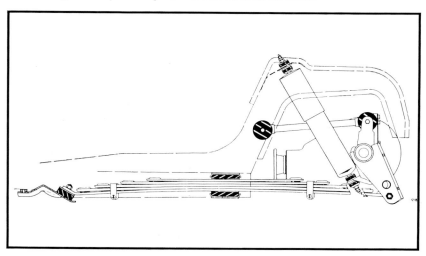

One of the more unusual features of the new 2.4 saloon was the difference in track between the front and rear wheels, the rear track being some 4⅜ inches narrower at only 4ft 2⅛″. This was apparently necessitated by the shape of the rear of the car and gave the vehicle a rather distinctive look – perhaps a little tail-heavy. A conventional hypoid rear axle was used with a ration of 4.55 to 1 on the manual/overdrive models, or 4.27 to 1 on the manual without overdrive and automatic transmission versions.

The car stood on 5-stud 15″ pressed steel wheels with 640 x 15 tubeless tyres (although other tyres could be specified to special order). Brake drums of 11⅛″ were used all round incorporating the Lockheed Brakemaster self-adjusting system which at the time Jaguar considered to be the ultimate in consistency of operation, the system comprising a master cylinder, 5½″ vacuum servo and the automatically adjusted front and rear brake assemblies. A pull-up type handbrake was situated on the floor at the right-hand side of the driver's seat operating on the rear wheels only.

Bodywork styling was both distinctive and modern in appearance owing much of its design to the other Jaguar models of the time. The monocoque principle offered great advantages in stiffness/weight ratios but rigidity was governed by the amount of "loose" areas – doors, windows, bonnet and boot openings, etc., or so it was thought at the time. Another big problem associated with unitary construction was noise , the cocoon of a monocoque making an excellent sounding board for the transmission of road noises. After a long period of experimentation, rubber mountings were extensively used (as mentioned earlier) to insulate the body from all aspects of noise and vibration. To maintain rigidity the car was based on two straight longitudinal members, running from the front suspension mountings to the rear spring anchorages housing the cantilevered springs, welded to provide a box section, together with several transverse box sections placed at the front of the body, underneath the scuttle, adjacent to the front suspension attachment points and beneath the front seats. Behind the rear seat structure reinforcement was via the wheel arches, seat pan and transverse pressings again. Body sills provided additional box sections to add stiffness to the overall shape. The ingenuity of the whole bodyshell was apparent by the all-up dry weight of only 25cwt.

Front end styling was remarkably similar to the XK sports car to the point of using similar bumpers, over-riders and the cast oval radiator grille. Chromium horn grilles were positioned either side of the main radiator grille close to the bumper, and inwardly placed headlamps, again in normal Jaguar fashion, were used. The horn grilles (only one of which was actually used for this purpose) were of the same design as on the Mark VIIM, as were the twin

2.4 styling mock-up.

Lucas foglamps sited on the front valance behind the bumper (a standard fitment on Special Equipment models). An unusual feature of the frontal styling was the fitment of oval side lights incorporating the indicator flashers set into the lower sections of the front wings as opposed to the normal Jaguar practice of sitting the side lights on top of the wings and using separate indicator flasher units.

The sides of the car were smooth, with little adornment, and again unusual for Jaguar at the time was the lack of the sweeping front wing line across the doors down to meet the rear wheel-arches. Instead, a gentle curve followed the waistline of the doors, sloping with the rear wing to meet the rear bumper. A chromium beading strip followed the line from the tapered edge of the bonnet to the rear bumper. The windscreen and rear window were relatively shallow and the four doors embodied quite substantial integrated window frames. Opening quarterlights were fitted to all doors, which had push-button Mazak door handles with the front pair lockable via the ignition key from the outside. Full spats covered the rear wheels in the same fashion as on the Mark VII, attached to the wheel-arches by Dutz fasteners totally concealed when the rear doors were closed. The rear wings tapered quite dramatically and the overall rear styling was again reminiscent of the bigger Mark VII with sloping boot and thick double-bar bumper. The rear number plate was centrally mounted on the boot lid (which opened upwards), having a chromium surround and Mazak reversing light and number plate light cover. Small tail-light clusters were sited either side of the boot lid at the base of the rear wings, as at the front embodying dual purpose side-light and indicator bulbs.

The overall effect was excellent, with a well proportioned design only lacking perhaps in window area, necessitated, or so it was thought at the time, to provide sufficient stiffness to the roof section. The 2.4 was, incidentally, never officially offered with a sun-roof because of such worries over rigidity, although later, when it was realised how well designed and strong the body was, a sun-roof became a frequent option chosen by many owners.

Consideration had been given to the size of the garage, the overall dimensions of the car being 15'3¾" long, 5'6¾" wide and 4'9½" high, or to put it another way, 16" shorter and 12" narrower than its big brother Mark VIIM. The 2.4 was also 8cwt lighter than the bigger saloon. The impressive appearance of the 2.4 styling disguised these compact dimensions and William Lyons had yet again proved his genius at design. Although the car was light at only 25cwt, one drawback seemed to be the excessive weight (over 55%) over the front wheels. This tended to make the steering heavy, as previously mentioned, and made the rear a little light, leading to instability at

Pre-production car still requiring front end styling amendments. Note the painted hub-caps, abandoned on production cars, and the holes at the top of the front wings indicating the possible fitment of Mark II-style side lights Also note the flush-mounted spot lights à la Mark II.

speed, often blamed on the narrow rear track although Jaguar claimed that this distribution of weight had been aimed at to create a satisfactory ride.

Despite the small dimensions, the body concealed a large 13½ cu. ft. boot with a flat floor, the spare wheel and tools hidden below the floor in a special well. Very early cars were equipped with a conventional tool roll with the bare amount of equipment, but soon after production got under way a specially designed, fully equipped tool box was fitted, shaped to fit snugly into the spare wheel centre. The boot provided very adequate accommodation for family luggage without the need to resort to roof-racks and the like. The boot floor was protected by a fitted hardura mat in grey, and a boot light was illuminated when the side-lights were switched on. On either side of the boot interior pre-formed board panels were fitted to protect the wing panels and to conceal the S.U. fuel pump on the nearside. Clipped to the rear of the boot were the jack and wheel brace, too large to be accommodated in the fitted tool kit. A twelve gallon fuel tank was sited underneath the boot, shaped around the spare wheel recess with the filler concealed under a hinged flap in the nearside rear wing.

Under the counterbalanced rear-hinged bonnet the six cylinder XK engine filled the compartment with little room left for ancillary equipment. The battery was situated near the bulkhead on the driver's side and was rather awkward to top up as the bonnet tended to get in the way. The heater box occupied the space on the opposite side of the bulkhead with the starter solenoid in the middle. The fuse box, cut-out, brake fluid reservoir and windscreen washer bottle were all placed against the inner wing panels. Although these items were easy to get at and service, other items such as the dipstick, oil filter and distributor were not, being literally buried in the engine compartment.

Interior passenger space, however, was not cramped and the 2.4 gave little away to its big brother Mark VII except perhaps in rear seat area. The leather seats were well proportioned, giving adequate leg room for both front and rear passengers. The front individual seats were of the bucket type and provided good lateral support for spirited driving (although a split bench-type was available as an option on manual gearbox cars, standard on automatic transmission models) and the rear bench type seat was adequate for three passengers abreast if necessary. Armrests were fitted to all doors and in the centre of the rear seat back, folding away into the seat back if necessary. Map pockets were fitted to all doors (which were trimmed in Rexine material) and the window frames were finished off with veneered wood fillets in true luxury tradition. In fact the whole interior of the new 2.4 epitomised Jaguar luxury at

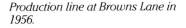
Production line at Browns Lane in 1956.

above
Impressive tool-kit supplied with the 2.4 and all subsequent variants of the model.

right
Dashboard of the Special Equipment model. The standard model (very rare) had no tachometer.

its best, and nothing was spared to ensure that the purchaser enjoyed the same attention to detail as the owner of the larger Jaguars. Deep pile carpets with underlay adorned the floor and the Vaumol leather upholstery was of excellent quality. Walnut veneer was used lavishingly on the dashboard, which was very workmanlike and impressively equipped. At either end of the dashboard, cubby hole glove boxes were fitted which provided useful storage space. On most models produced (to Special Equipment specification) the centre section of the dashboard was equipped with two large-diameter instruments, the rev. counter to the left (with integrated electric clock) and the speedometer to the right (with total mileage indicator and trip meter). To the left of the rev. counter was a much smaller gauge recording petrol level (with a neat red warning light to indicate low fuel level) and to the right of the speedometer a similarly size gauge recording oil pressure and water temperature. In the dead centre of the dashboard above the two larger instruments was the ammeter, below which the lighting switch was situated. At the base of the dashboard, switches were sited for (from left to right) windscreen wipers, heater booster fan, panel light switch, windscreen washer button (vacuum operated), interior light switch, ignition key switch, push button starter and cigar lighter. Underneath the dashboard there was a lever for the scuttle ventilator. Last but not least, to the left of the main instrument panel was a lever for the heater temperature adjustment, and to the right on the driver's side the manual choke lever. When overdrive was fitted a switch was sited on the driver's side easily to hand. On the top edge of the dashboard a convex interior mirror was fitted and twin sun visors were positioned above the windscreen. The flashing indicator switch was positioned on the steering column with a green tell-tale light. The headlamp dipswitch was floor mounted to the left of the clutch pedal. An interesting little item about the 2.4's interior concerns the siting of the ashtray for the front seat passenger and driver. William Lyons, being a non-smoker, did not consider the fitting of an ashtray necessary. However, pressure from his design team brought about a change of heart and an ashtray appeared, rather an afterthought, hidden behind a wood fillet underneath the dashboard just below the ignition switch. This subsequently proved a bad siting as key fobs attached to the ignition key dangled into the ashtray spreading ash everywhere; nevertheless the ashtray remained in this position unaltered until the introduction of the Mark II – perhaps Sir William had initiated his own anti-smoking campaign!

The 2.4 saloon was released to the public in October 1955 and was initially available in two forms, Standard and Special Equipment, both with manual transmission only. In Jaguar's own words from their 1955 brochure, "The Standard model, although fully equipped and carrying the same technical specification as the Special Equipment model, does not carry various items which many owners prefer either to dispense with or to add later according to their personal preference." How times have changed: it would be unthinkable today for a luxury car of the calibre of Jaguar to be offered without such basic items as a heating system or courtesy lights.

The Standard model is very rare today and it is not known exactly how many were built, but it was listed on the factory price lists right up to the end of the 2.4's production run in 1959, although it does not appear that many were sold after the initial launch. Is is clearly understandable why the Special Equipment model was so popular for a mere £21 more (excluding purchase tax). For this small extra sum the purchaser received a rev. counter, automatic

New 2.4s outside the Browns Lane offices awaiting despatch.

courtesy light switches operating when the doors were opened, a rear-seat armrest, cigar lighter, fresh-air ventilating and heater system, twin Lucas fog lamps, vacuum operated windscreen washers and even vitreous enamelled exhaust manifolds. Last but by no means least the Special Equipment specification included the unashamed luxury of a leaping Jaguar mascot on the leading edge of the bonnet. I have never seen a Standard model "in the flesh" and I doubt if any still exist today but with the Special Equipment model, what more could the sporting motorist of the day ask for?

Initial launch prices of the 2.4 litre saloon range in 1955 were:

Standard Saloon	£895 basic plus	£448.17s P. Tax	= £1343.17s
Std. with o/drive	£940 basic plus	£471.7s P.Tax	= £1411.7s
Special Equipment	£916 basic plus	£459.7s P. Tax	= £1375.7s
S.E. with o/drive	£961 basic plus	£481.17s P. Tax	= £1442.17s

The 2.4 was initially offered in a choice of ten body colours: Dove Grey, British Racing Green, Old English White, Birch Grey, Pastel Blue, Lavender Grey, Suede Green, Black, Battleship Grey and Pastel Green, with six options of interior trim colour – biscuit, tan, blue, green, red or grey. Right from the outset (as with other Jaguars) the 2.4 was available to special order in any colour to the customer's personal choice, with or without matching trim.

The car was released to the public at the Earls Court Motor Show of 1955 and initial reaction was excellent. The only real competition at this time amounted to the Armstrong Siddeley Sapphire 234 and 236, which were much dearer in price and lacked the finesse of the Jaguar's body style. The engines of the Armstrongs were also unsophisticated compared with the twin camshaft unit of the new 2.4 Jaguar. The only other major competitors in the small luxury saloon car field were the Daimler Conquest, Riley and Rover 90, all of which lacked the power of the Jaguar, its modern sporting looks and its value for money.

The 1955 Earls Court Motor Show 2.4.

Contemporary road-tests confirmed the public's reaction to the 2.4 litre Jaguar with such comments as "compact high performance and exceptional comfort at a medium price", "one of the most exciting small saloons around" and "offered at a reasonably low price for the high standards and quality construction for which the make is internationally respected." *Autosport*, after their road-test of the car on 14th December 1956, sent a telegram to Sir William Lyons reading, "Congratulations, your new 2.4 is the best all round car ever tested by *Autosport*" – praise indeed from the normally critical motoring press. The new car immediately found a niche in the marketplace and with glowing road-test reports was soon the success Jaguar had hoped for.

William Lyons eagerly awaited the opinion of the North American market but was slightly disappointed at their initial reaction. Although the car was generally very well received and the quality and reputation of Jaguar was not in question, the Americans felt the car lacked the performance they expected of the marque. Although out-and-out top speed was not that important (after all they had few unrestricted roads to maintain speeds of over 100mph) quick acceleration was imperative, and although no sluggard the 2.4 could not match the straight line acceleration of some of the big American V8s. As the car was not cheap, potential purchasers were not concerned with economy but preferred performance to a few extra miles per gallon. Nevertheless such comments in American magazines as "a more practical XK" and "a great road car" were common and apart from the lack of sufficient visibility and the slight shortage of power, the car was praised.

Contemporary English road-test performance figures showed the 2.4 to be a match for most European small cars with a 0 to 50mph time of 11 seconds, 0-60mph in 14.4 seconds, and a standing-start quarter mile time of 24.6 seconds. A maximum speed of over 101mph was recorded and the car could still maintain an average of over 18mpg in fuel consumption.

The 2.4 litre, reproduced from Jaguar's 1958 sales brochure.

The Jaguar 2.4 litre saloon was a masterpiece of engineering and a credit to Jaguar and its creator.

The 2·4 Litre Saloon

Improving the Breed

The 2.4 litre saloon was an economic miracle and that Jaguar were still producing such miracles more than thirteen years later when the 2.4's latterday equivalent (the 240) cost a mere £21 more than its predecessor in 1956 is common knowledge. The original car, however, was not without its vices. Apart from the North American complaints about lack of power there were other more down-to-earth faults to be rectified. For instance the Panhard rod had a habit of breaking away from its mounting point and although reinforced in May of 1956, the problem was never totally eliminated even at the close of production of the series in 1969. The standard shock absorbers did not last long either, and on the early cars there was a tendency for the rear springs to loosen. Nevertheless the car was very successful and for Jaguar, as this was a breakthrough in design, it is surprising that more serious problems did not arise.

It did not take Jaguar long to realise the possibilities of improving the performance of the 2.4 litre and therefore not long after production commenced a set of tuning packages was made available. Although it is not known exactly how many of these special tuning kits were sold most may well have gone to North American buyers. A tuning modification booklet was available from Jaguar outlining the improvements which could be made, and the kits were available in three separate stages depending on how far the owner wished to go in improving the maximum power of his car, although, as Jaguar pointed out, at the loss of some low speed performance. In standard trim the maximum power output of the 2.4 litre engine was 112bhp at 5,750rpm. With the Stage One modifications the power output was raised to 119bhp at 5,800rpm; for this changes included modifying the carburettors by fitting flat type throttle spindles, 26mm chokes, 120 main jets, 190 air correction jets and 60 pump jets. The fitting of NA8 spark plugs was advised along with the removal of the existing exhaust system silencer, replacing same with a straight-through version (part number C.1872) which called for the extension of the existing tail-pipe by approximately 6" to meet up with the shortened silencer, and a slight reduction in the diameter of the tail-pipe at the silencer unit. In addition to this it was also necessary to cut off the short entrance pipe from both the discarded silencer and the new one, welding the one removed from the old unit onto the new unit. It is interesting to note that Jaguar made the comment in the instructions relating to the changeover of exhaust system that "an increase in the level of exhaust noise is to be expected" – I wonder if this made the 2.4 sound like an XK! The total cost of the conversion to Stage One amounted to £3.8s.0d (plus tax). Further changes were suggested by Jaguar complementary to the Stage One tune, amounting to fitting a twin pipe exhaust system, a close-ratio gearbox (where not already fitted), a higher ratio steering box, part number C.12212 rhd or C.12213 lhd (a frequently fitted option for competition use), and the fitting of stiffer setting dampers (part number C.12692 front and C.12693 rear), all at extra cost.

The Stage Two tuning kit increased the power output to 131bhp at 5,900rpm, the modifications amounting to the Stage One improvements mentioned in the last paragraph along with the addition of high lift camshafts (part number C.13080 inlet and C.13081 exhaust). Also new valve springs and distributor were required, bringing the total cost to £18.6s.3d. As with Stage One, Jaguar also recommended the extra options of a close-ratio gearbox, high ratio steering and suspension modifications to further improve the overall capabilities of the car.

The ultimate 'mod' was Stage Three, which brought the power output up to 150bhp at 6,000rpm and recommended far more severe changes to the specification. At this stage of tune the cylinder head was replaced with the "B" type as fitted to the XK140, complete with inlet manifold and twin 1¾" S.U. carburettors, discarding the under-carburated Solex downdraught type. This also meant blanking off the dashboard mounted manual choke lever as the S.U.s were equipped with an auxiliary starting carburettor. The air cleaner had to be changed along with the distributor, and due to the higher engine torque a new clutch cover assembly (part number 7018) incorporating stronger thrust springs was needed. The other major alteration to attain Stage Three tune was the fitting of a twin pipe exhaust system, necessary at this stage rather than a suggested modification as at Stage One or Two. These Stage Three modifications would set the owner back £225.8s.1d (again plus tax).

The other suggested changes for Stage One and Two tune would have cost the following in 1956:

Twin pipe exhaust system	**£17.1s.10d**	
Close-ratio gearbox	**£26.5s.4d**	(optional Stage Three also)
High-ratio steering box	**£8.16s.11d**	(optional Stage
Suspension mods	**£15.3s.**	Three also

The net total cost therefore to obtain the very best from the 2.4 litre unit in performance and driveability using factory recommended options would have been £275.13s.4d bringing the total cost of the Special Equipment model to £1,236 (excluding purchase tax).

Whilst on the subject of prices, the Jaguar 2.4 saw its first price increase in October 1956 to:

Standard Saloon	**£953** basic plus **£477.12s** tax = **£1430.17s** total.
Special Equipment Saloon	**£976** basic plus **£489.7s** tax = **£1465.7s** total.

Laycock de Normanville overdrive cost a further £45 (plus £22.10s purchase tax) on either model.

Although no major changes in design were made to the 2.4 saloon during its production, many minor modifications were carried out, and these will be highlighted later in this chapter. There was, however, one major development from the 2.4 which took place in February 1957 when Jaguar introduced an entirely new version, the larger engined 3.4 litre (3,442cc) car. It is astonishing to think that despite a major fire that devastated production at the beginning of that February at Browns Lane, Jaguar were still able to produce two hundred 2.4s and 3.4s by the beginning of March.

The new 3.4 was very similar to its smaller engined sister but was offered with the XK140 engine, complete with "B" type cylinder head. Twin S.U. carburettors were fitted as standard and the new engine developed a staggering 210bhp at 5,500rpm. The larger engine necessitated the fitting of modified engine bearers and a larger radiator block as well as stiffer front coil springs (14 9/16" as opposed to 14" on the 2.4) to cope with the extra weight over the front wheels. The manual with overdrive Moss gearbox remained unchanged but for the first time an automatic transmission option was available from Borg Warner. This automatic gearbox was of the conventional three speed type but instead of utilising a steering column mounted lever to select the gears as was usual on cars of this period, a small stubby Bakelite handle was situated in the centre of the car just below the dashboard. Siting the quadrant selector in this position meant that no modifications were necessary for left or right hand drive models, Jaguar clearly expecting to sell

The 3.4 automatic transmission model. Note the extra-large brake pedal, and the transmission selector quadrant in the centre of the dashboard.

The 3.4 litre engine, considered by many to be the sweetest of the XK range.

many automatic transmission models abroad. In common with other automatic transmission Jaguars of this time, an intermediate speed hold was fitted, actuated by a fascia mounted switch in the place of the overdrive switch on manual transmission cars. The automatic gearbox was longer than the conventional Moss box and required the use of a divided propshaft. A Salisbury 4HA axle was used on both manual and automatic versions.

The other mechanical change carried out with the introduction of the 3.4 amounted to substituting the single pipe exhaust system for a twin-pipe system, this time emerging from the offside corner.

Externally the body shape was the same as the 2.4s, but was instantly recognisable from the side by the fitting of smart cut-away spats over the rear wheels, replacing the full spats. In most respects these new spats gave a better and more sporting line to the 3.4 although emphasising the narrow rear track quite considerably. It was hoped that they would help cool the rear drum brakes, a minor concession to the increased performance. The new spats subsequently became a standard fitting on all compact saloons in production.

From the rear the only departure from the 2.4 was a discreet 3.4 badge on the boot lid (although on some cars leaving the factory even this was omitted). 3.4s were, however, still recognisable from the rear by the twin exhaust pipes.

From the frontal aspect the changes were more numerous. Because of the larger radiator block a new wider grille was needed to aid cooling, this time not cast and with narrower slats. A 3.4 litre badge was inserted into the top of the grille in the same fashion as on the 2.4 car. Using the wider grille necessitated the fitting of slightly modified front wings. Missing from the front, at least initially, were the matching Lucas foglamps, listed during the first few months as an optional extra but later re-adopted as standard, although never so on cars destined for the U.S.A. and certain other export markets.

Unfortunately, amidst all the changes made on the 3.4, drum brakes remained exactly as on the 2.4, and *Autocar* in its road-test of the 3.4 on 1st March 1957 actually commented, "This is the type of vehicle which, in due course, will lend itself to the fitting of disc brakes." In reality very few drum braked 3.4s left the factory, as Sir William Lyons was at the time working on a disc braked version, and disc brakes were offered shortly after the car's release as an optional extra on all four wheels for a mere £37 and were specified by the majority of buyers.

The disc brake system, manufactured by Dunlop, consisted of four caliper-type disc brakes hydraulically controlled by means of a foot operated master cylinder and vacuum servo unit. The discs were 11⅜" in diameter and the servo was manufactured by Lockheed. The system utilised round friction pads and, unfortunately, it was necessary to take the wheel cylinders off to change the pads. Because this was time-consuming and meant that the system had to be bled each time, it was said that some owners neglected their brakes until work was absolutely necessary, causing excessive wear to the discs. The handbrake worked on separate calipers on the rear discs. The new Dunlop disc brakes were a revelation to Jaguar owners, working exceptionally well. Competition drivers at the time thought very highly of the new system and Ivor Bueb (the racing driver of high repute) commented, "The success of Dunlop disc brakes in motor racing is well known but everyday experience with them on the new Jaguar convinces me that this is the braking system of the future for all vehicles. What appeals to me is not only their power but the

Frontal aspect of the 3.4 Mark I (note the lack of mascot on this export model). This clearly shows the wider grille.

*Early Mark I 2.4 with the narrow, cast grille and
full rear spats.*

*The Mark II engine compartment was
well filled.*

The author's early (1959) 3.4 litre Mark II.

*A rare gathering of the whole Mark I and II range,
from early 2.4 Mark I to the 340/380 model.*

*Front view of the 3.4 Mark II. The subsequent 340
had thinner bumpers.*

Rare picture of the original type front wing section alongside the later type, showing the difference in the grille aperture.

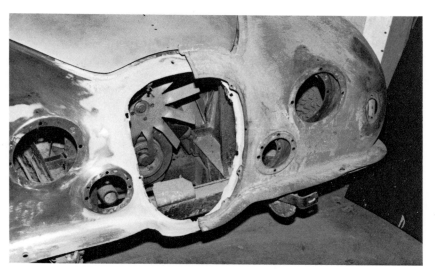

Rare picture of the original type front wing section alongside the later type, showing the difference in the grille aperture.

smooth and progressive braking action they give. I really believe they are an absolute necessity for all fast cars." Mike Hawthorn (another famous Jaguar racing driver of the time) also concluded, "With the new 3.4 litre Jaguar which gives me such superb motoring on the road I know I can drive with full confidence as the high performance of the car is matched by the most powerful and reliable brakes in the world."

Internally, the 3.4 was exactly the same as the 2.4, save for the lack of a choke mixture control on the dashboard (replaced by a chrome fillet) and the already mentioned automatic transmission quadrant. When automatic transmission was specified a new split-bench seat was fitted to the front, this feature later becoming an option on all models including the manual 2.4 litre car.

The 3.4 litre was Jaguar's first 120mph saloon and as such carried a great deal of prestige for the company. It was no sluggard on acceleration, despite the weight of 27cwt (2cwt more than the smaller engined version). With a 0-50 mph time of 7 seconds, a 0 to 60mph time of 9.1 seconds and a 0 to 100mph time of 26 seconds, the 3.4 was actually two seconds faster than an XK120 with the "C" Type cylinder head! The standing start quarter mile was covered in just over 17 seconds and up to 19mpg was possible. The automatic transmission model was also an excellent performer, with a 0 to 50mph time of 8.7 seconds, a 0 to 60mph time of 11.2 seconds, and the standing start quarter mile in a little over 18 seconds.

The world's motoring press were very enthusiastic about the new car, their comments including: "The most important addition to Britain's high-performance export market," from *Autosport*, "It is no exaggeration to describe the new 3.4 litre Jaguar both outright and in terms of value for money as one of the most outstanding cars in current production anywhere," from *Autocar*, and "Fundamentally, this is a car which has few superiors in respect of providing smooth, quiet and comfortable travel for five people, yet which has speed and acceleration of the most remarkable order," from *Motor*.

Comment from the valued North American market was just as good. The new 3.4 was just what they wanted, providing superb performance. In fact it was one of the fastest saloons available in the world at the time. Aside from the all-out performance the Americans were taken aback by the smoothness, silence and flexibility of the engine. With increased power and flexibility, along with the option of disc brakes on all four wheels and automatic transmission, the 3.4 could now be used to its full extent without fear of critcism of any kind. The 3.4 car virtually had the market to itself, the Americans having nothing at all like the small compact Jaguar. Even their own home-bred Cadillacs, Buicks and Thunderbirds could not match the exhilarating performance of the 'cat'.

On the English scene the competition really only amounted to the Riley 2.6 litre saloon, although on acceleration, outright top speed and engineering this was no match for the Jaguar. Most of the other British 2½ to 3½ litre saloons were not at all sporting by nature, or were much bigger and therefore competed with the larger Mark VII and VIII Jaguar saloons. The 3.4 litre Jaguar was truly a sporting saloon and was a match for most sports cars of the time, becoming the obvious choice in competition circles, where it gained the respect of many famous drivers. As already mentioned, Ivor Bueb and Mike Hawthorn were ardent admirers of the new 3.4, being among the first to purchase examples, along with Roy Salvadori and Duncan Hamilton.

Prices for the new 3.4 litre saloons were:

Manual model	**£1114** basic plus **£558.7s** p.tax = **£1672.7s**
Auto transmission model	**£1242** basic plus **£622.6s** p.tax = **£1864.7s**
Manual/overdrive model	**£1159** basic plus **£580.17s** p.tax = **£1739.17s**

Normal optional extras included:-

Disc brakes	**£45.10s** basic plus **£12.5s** p.tax = **£57.15s**
Wire wheels	**£35.00** basic plus **£17.10s** p.tax = **£52.10s**

By October of 1957 the 2.4 model had increased in price to:

Standard model	**£996** basic plus **£499.7s** p.tax = **£1495.7s**
Special Equipment model	**£1019** basic plus **£510.17s** p.tax = **£1529.17s**
S.E. Overdrive model	**£1064** basic plus **£533.7s** p.tax = **£1597.7s**
Automatic model	**£1139** basic plus **£570.17s** p.tax = **£1709.17s**

As with the 3.4 disc brakes and wire wheels were available as extra cost options.

The Duke of Kent (nearest car) taking delivery of his new 3.4 in 1958 from Lofty England (middle) and Michael Christie.

Both models remained in production without any major modifications although many minor changes were made to improve on the basic design. All the known alterations are listed below along with, wherever possible, chassis or engine numbers.

Very early on in the production of the 2.4, in fact at chassis number 900207 rhd and 940014 lhd, the spare wheel clamp was modified (part number BD11007 replacing number BD10636), although no reason for this is shown in the factory records. On 21st December 1955 the cylinder head was modified by the reduced depth of tapped holes for studs on the inlet face. The new part number was C.6733/1 commencing at engine number BB.1001. At the same time the choke indicator plate was altered with new lettering (part number BD11802), both these items commencing at chassis number 900351 rhd and 940020 lhd. At around the same time the front road springs were replaced by a new type being one-quarter of an inch longer (part number C.8924/1 replacing number C.8924).

In March 1956, from chassis number 90522 rhd and 940020 lhd the brake master cylinder and reservoir were modified (part number C.12184 replacing number C.8955). The difference in the two assemblies amounted to the angle at which the reservoir was attached to the cylinder in relation to the mounting studs. When fitted, the original type has the reservoir filler cap immediately in front of the cylinder; the later type has the cap situated to the right of cylinder.

In April 1956 at chassis number 900822 rhd and 940207 lhd, the heater intake duct was modified to provide a straighter run for the rev. counter cable. According to Service Bulletin No. 184, this "modification" was made by simply indenting the heater duct! Simple but apparently effective. After complaints about "flat spots" in low speed acceleration the following modifications were recommended to the Solex carburettors:

The 2.4/3.4 production line at Browns Lane in late 1957.

Part No. 4984	Choke Tube	24mm	replacing 25mm
Part No. 4977	Air Correction Jet	180	replacing 160
Part No. 4989	Needle Valve	1.5mm	replacing 2.0mm

In the same month the list of colour schemes for the 2.4 was increased to cover Pearl Grey, Pacific Blue, Carmine Red, Arbor Green and Maroon (with the same match of interior trim as before). Lastly in April at chassis number 900862 rhd and 940210 lhd (plus odd vehicles before), the bolts securing the drive gear to the differential case were increased in size from ⅜″ to ⁷⁄₁₆″.

In May 1956 the Jaguar factory asked all dealers to modify the Panhard rod mounting. Apparently some cases of breakage of the bracket securing the Panhard rod to the body had been notified. Dealers were asked to inspect all cars and if it was found they were to carry out the necessary welding to ensure that the fault would not recur. In June of that year the rear axle ratio on non-overdrive cars was altered to 4.27 to 1 from 4.55 to 1 (overdrive models retained the 4.55 to 1 ratio). This modification took place from chassis number 901582 rhd and 940606 lhd. Around the same time, due to a few complaints from owners about clutch slip or difficulty experienced in obtaining the necessary free travel at the clutch pedal, a stronger return spring C.5120 (from the Mark VII saloon) was fitted along with the spring plate C.5178 and shakeproof washer C.726. This modification took place at chassis number 901592 rhd and 940569 lhd (plus a few earlier examples). Later in that month a modified type of speedometer cable with fluted outer cable and a nylon insert at one end of the inner cable was used, effective from chassis number 901482 rhd and 940560 lhd (non-overdrive cars) and 901561 rhd and 940580 lhd (overdrive models).

In June 1956 Jaguar announced the fitting of a vibration damper to the front end of the crankshaft from engine number BB.2500. This damper was of Metalastic construction and was fitted to all subsequent engines although it was not suggested that dealers recall earlier cars for the modification. In the same month Jaguar announced that earlier non-overdrive cars could now have overdrive fitted as a factory option. The overdrive system was available as a kit for the princely sum of £81.3s with an additional labour cost of £32.10s when fitted at Jaguar's own Service Department. Everything required for the modification was supplied in the kit even down to the dashboard mounted switch, although when fitted to cars after chassis number 901582 rhd or 940606 lhd, a change of axle assembly was necessary, returning the ratio to 4.55 to 1; the extra cost here would have been £21 exchange.

Jaguar had received some complaints from owners about oil working up the speedometer cable and because of this a modified speedometer drive assembly (part number C.12256) incorporating a lip type rubber seal was supplied. A few complaints had also been received about appreciable water loss from the cooling system. No positive cure was found although Jaguar

The plush rear-seating arrangement of the Mark I saloon.

The only tell-tale of a true Mark I
rear seat back – the stitched centre
section above the centre arm-rest.

advised dealers to check that the domed cylinder head nuts were properly threaded and that the radiator filler cap was sealing correctly.

From the 23rd July 1956 cars fitted with an overdrive unit received a close-ratio gearbox (part number BB5691) from chassis number 903163 rhd and 941252 lhd. In September 2.4 litre cars from chassis number 902169 rhd and 940973 lhd received a new type of coil spring rear engine mounting C.12298 (or C.12299 for overdrive cars). Around the same time a revised rear road spring front mounting plate was fitted (C.12343) consisting of a one piece pressing fitted in place of the fabricated type.

In September from engine number BB.3118, a new type Solex carburettor was fitted incorporating a weir in the float chamber. In the same month Jaguar advised a change in ignition static timing on 8 to 1 compression engines from 10° to 6° B.T.D.C. Also due to customer complaints about leakage, copper washers were fitted to the sump strainer cover plate (from engine number BB.5024). Other complaints were received about knocking or cracking noises from the rear springs; in view of this Jaguar fitted modified springs incorporating synthetic rubber to the ends of the spring leaves (the spring part numbers remained unchanged). This modification took effect from chassis number 902882 rhd and 941156 lhd.

In October Jaguar received complaints about the modified weir type Solex carburettors to the effect that engines were cutting out when taking bends at high speeds. Dealers were advised to drill a 2.5 mm hole through the weir in order to effect a cure. In the same month Jaguar started to fit modified dampers (C.8923 front and C.8926 rear) from chassis number 904285 rhd and 941631 lhd.

Early in November, at chassis number 90561 rhd and 941767 lhd, a shroud was fitted to the scuttle ventilator aperture to prevent water seeping behind the instrument panel. At engine number BB.7113 the main jets in the carburettors were amended in size from 115 to 110, and from engine number BB.9001 a pressed steel sump was fitted (C.9155) instead of the cast aluminium type. Oil capacity remained unchanged at 13 pints but a new dipstick (C.12620) was used incorporating a "knurled section" for oil level identification.

Moving on now to 1957, some dealers had been approached about the possibility of fitting a lockable lid to the petrol filler. Jaguar responded by suggesting the fitting of a Mark VII petrol filler lock and the making up of a striker plate to suit! At chassis number 906247 rhd and 941930 lhd a check valve was fitted in the vacuum line between the inlet manifold and the brake servo attached to the inlet manifold studs (part number C.12790).

Some fuel starvation had been reported and Jaguar suggested drilling a 1.5mm hole through the top of the filler cap to aid venting. Also, early in January 1957 Jaguar made available additional exterior colour schemes for the 2.4. Maroon became a slightly different shade and was renamed Imperial Maroon, and a deeper Claret colour was added along with Sherwood Green, Indigo Blue and Cotswold Blue.

In February 1957 Jaguar announced a modification to the hydraulic dampers, using a high setting (part Nos. C.12692 front and C.12693 rear) from chassis numbers 906500 rhd and 941985 lhd. Also from engine number BB.9657 modified camshafts with a hole drilled through the base of each cam into the main oilway were used in an attempt to reduce tappet noise when starting from cold. (Camshaft numbers were C.13082 inlet and C.13083 exhaust.)

At this time Jaguar were still receiving complaints from owners about noises from the rear springs. In a further attempt to rectify this problem Service Bulletin No. 210 was issued stating, ". . . the upper spring mounting clamps should be examined for distortion. If any distortion exists this should be rectified and in addition support brackets (C.12779) should be fitted and welded between the spring mounting clamp and the spring reinforcing channel."

In May of that year a new radiator unit was fitted (part no. C.12672) with a separate filler and inlet pipe of the same type as already used on the 3.4 litre car. This modification took effect from chassis number 906964 rhd and 942182 lhd. In the same month, from chassis number 906949 and 942190, a revised type of voltage regulator was used (part no. C.8821).

In July a modified oil filter was fitted to 2.4 and 3.4 litre cars commencing at engine numbers BC.2256 (2.4) and KE.3054 (3.4). The new style filter had a dome nut to retain the oil pressure relief valve and had a straight outlet adaptor for the hose to the sump. A modified blanking plate was used with a "dimple" to ensure that it could not be fitted the wrong way round. In the same month a new type (stronger) wiper motor was fitted to all cars commencing at chassis numbers 907359 2.4 rhd, 942311 2.4 lhd, 970327 3.4 rhd and 986134 3.4 lhd. The new motor's part number was C.13503 rhd and C.13504 lhd.

In September 1957 all cars received a modified smaller dynamo pulley from engine numbers BC.2959 (2.4) and KE.3888 (3.4), effectively increasing the dynamo rotation speed. A shortened fan belt was needed.

Jaguar were still receiving reports of knocking noises from the rear of the car and it was found that on 3.4 litre cars and 2.4s fitted with the handbrake compensator, under full bump conditions it was possible for the compensator to foul the bottom of the boot floor. Jaguar suggested to dealers that they cut out a ¼" strip of metal to reduce the height of the compensator bracket.

Still in September of 1957 Jaguar announced the fitting of an air cleaner to the air intake of the 6 ⅞" brake servo on both the 2.4 and 3.4. From chassis number 907974 rhd and 942465 lhd, 2.4 litre models received the 3.4 litre style enlarged radiator grille necessitating, as with the 3.4, modified front wings and air intake for the air cleaner behind the grille. At the same time (from engine no. BC.3161), 2.4s were fitted with a petrol filter, part number C.13681, of the glass bowl type with a flat filter gauze.

On 13th November all models became available with a new interior trim colour, suede green, taking effect from body number 12477. From engine number BC.3600 (2.4) and KE.4856 (3.4) Jaguar fitted a revised type oil pressure relief valve. A stop pin was fitted to the centre of the spring limiting the travel of the valve. Also, at engine numbers BC.3699 (2.4) and KE.4964 (3.4) synthetic rubber bonded chain dampers replaced the nylon type. In the same month from chassis number 908095 2.4 rhd and 942483 2.4 lhd, 970948 3.4 rhd and 986592 3.4 lhd a modified 5½″ brake servo was used introducing an adjustable type of push-rod. This modification only affected drum braked cars.

At this time automatic transmission became available on the 2.4 litre models. Basically of the same design as used on other Jaguars at the time, a new type of torque converter was used, the difference being in the direct drive plate fitted. The "special" 2.4 litre unit was marked by pink paint markings on the convertor. Around the same time (although no details are known from factory records), 2.4s started to leave the production area adopting the modified 3.4 style cut-away rear wheel spats.

In 1958 modifications continued with the introduction of a modified thermostat (part number C.13944) from engine number BC.4408 (2.4) and KE.5733 (3.4). To suit this modification, the bore in the outlet pipe was increased by .25mm. Also in January ready-prepared kits became available to convert drum braked cars to disc brakes. Other kits were also available to convert disc wheeled cars to wire wheels. The kits available were as follows:

Kit A – to convert drum brakes to disc brakes. Part No. 7389	**£100**
Kit B – to convert drum brakes to disc brakes and disc wheels to wire wheels. Part No. 7390	**£180**
Kit C – to convert disc wheels to wire wheels. Part No. 7391	**£83**

At this time chromium plated wire wheels would also cost an extra £7.19s.6d. Although everything else was included in the above kits, for the earlier 2.4 litre models the new-style cut-away rear wheel spats were necessary at a further extra cost of £4.2s (for the pair).

By this time production cars had already been fitted with a cast iron brake master cylinder body replacing the previous aluminium type and in conjunction with this change an unhardened piston was fitted to the master cylinder. Also at this time a further exterior colour scheme was added to the now lengthy range – Forest Green. All colours remained unchanged although by this time no less than three distinct paint mixes of Pearl Grey had already been used!

In February of 1958 drum braked cars had a larger 6⅞″ vacuum servo fitted necessitating also the change of brake pedal and clutch pedal housing, effective from chassis number 909061 2.4 rhd, 942677 2.4 lhd, 971732 3.4 rhd and 987406 3.4 lhd. In the same month progressive bump stops were fitted to the front suspension on all models from chassis number 909536 2.4 rhd, 942729 2.4 lhd, 972037 3.4 rhd and 987685 3.4 lhd.

Several complaints had been received of the handbrake cross cables fouling the rear wheel-arch when cars were fully laden or under strong power, applicable to disc braked cars only. A modified inner pad carrier and lever were made available for all cars from chassis number 910118 2.4 rhd, 942854 2.4 lhd, 972401 3.4 rhd and 988216 3.4 lhd. New cross cables and compensator bracket were also used, and to provide adequate clearance for the compensator in its new position it was necessary to cut out on the longitudinal depressions in the boot floor and weld in a new plate (part no.7481). The flange of the chassis side member had also to be knocked out flush with the box section.

In May the rear road springs received further attention with the fitting of a new type (C.10791/1), the difference being a change in free camber. In July the

dashboard mounted overdrive switch was altered from an illuminated plastic type to a conventional metal toggle-switch and on 11th September a new style remote gear lever was fitted from body number D16173 (2.4) and E010054 (3.4) replacing the previous 'cranked' version. In the same month, on 2.4 litre cars from chassis number 911658 rhd and 943149 lhd, an oil bath air cleaner became a standard fitting (part no. C.14213). The air cleaner was fitted on top of the cylinder head with a pipe running forward towards the radiator for air intake. Around the same time new 60 watt headlamp bulbs were introduced for all models, home and export, in right hand drive form.

In November 1958 modified Girling hydraulic dampers were fitted giving consistent damping at all operating temperatures. These were part numbers C.14586 (front) and C.14587 (rear), apparently fitted at various times to the front and rear on the production line, from chassis numbers 911522 2.4 rhd front, 812637 2.4 rhd rear, 943124 2.4 lhd front, 975162 3.4 lhd rear, 973987 3.4 rhd front, 975162 3.4 rhd rear, 989137 3.4 lhd front and 990178 3.4 lhd rear.

At the same time disc braked cars received revised attachment for the rear caliper adaptor plate – bolts, shakeproof washers and nuts were superseded by longer bolts and self-locking nuts. In the same month a new 12 bladed radiator cooling fan was fitted and the fan cowl used with the previous 4 bladed fan was dispensed with, replaced by a fan shield at the top of the radiator. Part numbers were fan (C.12391), shield (C.14732), fitted from chassis number 915349 2.4 rhd and 943118 2.4 lhd.

On 1st January 1959 a quite substantial and important change was made

Intermediate styling of the 2.4, still with full rear wheel spats but with wider radiator grille.

by the fitting of new Dunlop bridge type calipers with "quick change" disc brake pads to all models. This enabled the pads to be removed without dismantling the wheel cylinders, a very worthwhile modification. The modification became effective from chassis numbers 913144 2.4 rhd disc wheels, 913234 2.4 rhd wire wheels, 943331 2.4 lhd disc wheels, 943343 2.4 lhd wire wheels, 975688 3.4 rhd disc wheels, 975783 3.4 rhd wire wheels, 990694 3.4 lhd disc wheels and 990795 3.4 lhd wire wheels. At the same time new 72 spoke wire wheels were adopted to replace the original 60 spoke type, making the wheels much stronger. Wire wheeled cars destined for Germany received new style non-eared knock-on hubs falling in line with revised legislation. Also in January, from engine number BC.8075 (2.4) and KF.2501 (3.4), a vacuum reservoir was incorporated in the line between the inlet manifold and the servo. The reservoir tank was fitted underneath the offside front wing forward of the front offside wheel. A vacuum check valve was fitted with a hose from the inlet manifold (to the longer check valve connection) and another hose to the servo. Modified ball joints with a larger diameter ball and an increased angle of movement were fitted to all models around this time. The ball joint bolt hole centres in the upper wishbone levers and packing pieces were also increased from 1 11/16″ to 1¾″. Chassis numbers affected were 912622 2.4 rhd drum braked, 912744 2.4 rhd disc braked, 943267 2.4 lhd drum braked, 943288 2.4 lhd disc braked, 975232 3.4 rhd and 990270 3.4 lhd. Finally, in January 1959, 60 watt headlamp bulbs were modified for left hand drive cars.

In April 1959 the steering mechanism on all models was slightly modified, a re-designed steering box and idler assembly (part numbers C.14845 rhd and C.14846 lhd steering unit and C.14887 idler assembly). The new steering unit was lower geared and gave approximately 4¼ turns lock to lock. The change took effect from chassis number 914564 2.4 rhd, 943496 2.4 lhd, 976917 3.4 rhd and 991866 3.4 lhd. At the same time lead indium big end bearings were fitted to all 2.4 and 3.4 litre engines (part no. C.5893). Effective engine numbers were BE.1116 (2.4) and KF.6219 (3.4)

In May 1959 the oil filter blanking plate (part no. C.12803) previously mentioned earlier in this chapter was no longer used – no reason being given in the factory records. In the same month a new 25 amp dynamo and replacement voltage regulator were fitted, effective from chassis number 913953 2.4 rhd, 943437 2.4 lhd, 977762 3.4 rhd and 992494 3.4 lhd. During June of that year a more efficient rear hub seal was fitted to eliminate leaks and an electrically driven rev. counter replaced the cable driven variety, this modification falling in line with all other Jaguar models of the period.

The only other known modifications carries out during the production period concern the 3.4 litre cars only. In April 1958 Dunlop RS4 tyres replaced the RS3s as standard equipment, and in November the new 12 bladed radiator fan was fitted as mentioned earlier with the 2.4 litre cars. Earlier, in May 1957, left hand drive cars from chassis number 985600 had the aperture for the radiator grille made slightly smaller and a modified grille was fitted to suit. This modified grille also had a five-stud fixing and not four-stud as on earlier cars. (All right hand drive cars already had the new style grille fitted). Also in May, 3.4 litre engines received a new carburettor needle, LB replacing LB1.

Owners, particularly of 3.4s, were *still* complaining of knocks from the rear end. Jaguar found that on most cars prior to chassis 970592 rhd and 986301 lhd the rear axle cover plate could foul the body, giving rise to a knock under fully laden conditions or heavy acceleration. Instructions were given to dealers to "modify" this plate by flattening it under local heat!

In September 1957 a more efficient anti-creep solenoid was fitted to 3.4 automatics (part number C.12750). At engine number KE.3025 (plus a few earlier engines), longer inlet valve guides were fitted. The new valve guides (part no.C7260) were 1 $^{13}/_{16}$" long as opposed to 1½". At chassis numbers 970877 rhd and 986554 lhd, the 3.4 litre cars received modified silencers, although no particulars of what the modifications amounted to are disclosed in the factory records. In November, however, further modifications are noted at chassis number 971503 rhd and 987132 lhd. The stub pipes at the front of the silencers (part no. C.13578/1 and C.13578/2) were increased in length by 2". To suit this modification the down pipes were shortened in length by 2" and the suffix /1 added to the appropriate part number. At the same time, at chassis number 971637 rhd and 987293 lhd, an oil bath air cleaner was fitted, at which time carburettor needles were altered from TL to SC. Finally, at some time in 1957 the interior rear-view mirror was repositioned and attached to the roof instead of the top facia rail.

In May 1958 automatic transmission 3.4s from engine number KE.7052 received a modification to the valve block incorporated to eliminate the possibility of a jerk when a closed throttle downshift between intermediate and low gears took place.

In January 1959, at engine number KF.2501, a new ½" fan belt was fitted and pulleys altered to suit.

During the production run of the 2.4 and 3.4 litre compact Jaguars an enormous range of extras were on offer to the proud Jaguar owner. Apart from the items covered in this chapter so far, further accessories were available as follows:

Item	Basic price	P.Tax	Total Cost
Radiomobile 200 manual radio	£36.2s.3d	£18.1s.2d	£54.3s.5d
Ekco push button radio	£43.9s	£21.14s.6d	£65.3s.6d
Extension radio speaker with changeover switch	£5.10s	£2.15s	£8.5s
Ace Silver Peak number plates	£3.5s.6d	£1.12s.9d	£4.18s.3d
Chromium GB plate	£1.10s	15s	£2.5s
Roof mounted radio aerial	£6.12s.6d	£3.6s.3d	£7.12s.6d
Laminated windscreen	£5.5s	£2.12s.6d	£7.12s.6d
Set of 4 Rimbellishers	£8	£4	£12
Ace Turbo wheeltrims (5)	£7	£3.10s	£10.10s
Witter tow bar	£7	£3.10s	£10.10s
Standard Exide Battery	£3.3s	£1.11s.6d	£4.14s.6d
Double Life Exide battery	£5.5s	£2.12s.6d	£7.17s6d

Item	Price 1	Price 2	Price 3
Le Mans headlamps 40/45watt	£2.2s	£1.1s	£3.3s
Desmo rally lamp	£5.5s	£2.12s.6d	£7.17s.6d
Locking petrol filler cap	£2.2s	£1.1s	£3.3s
Bracket to raise drivers seat by 1"	£3.3s	£1.11s.6d	£4.14s.6d
Split bench seat (standard on automatic transmission cars)	£5.5s	£2.12s.6d	£7.17s.6d
Delaney Gallay RKN safety belt for front seat passenger	£3.3s	£1.11s.6d	£4.14s.6d
KL radiator blind	£4.10s	£2.5s	£6.15s
Loose replacement leather seat panels	7/2d per square foot		
Loose touch-up paint	6/6d per pint		
Bulk loose paint	£4.13s per gallon		
Goodyear Eagle tyres	£16.12s.6d	£8.6s.3d	£24.18s.9d
Town and Country rear tyres	£3.15s	£1.17s.6d	£5.12s.6d
Dunlop Weathermaster rear tyres	£1.5s	12/6d	£1.17s.6d
Lifeguard tubes	£17.12s.6d	£8.16s.3d	£26.8s.9d
Whitewall tyres (set of 5)	£8	£4	£12
Michelin 'X' tyres (complete with recalibrated speedometer)	£10.12s.6d	£5.6s.3d	£15.18s.9d
Dunlop Fort Tubeless tyres	£10.10s	£5.5s	£15.15s
Durabank tyres (with tubes)	£6.2s.6d	£3.1s.3d	£9.3s.9d
India Super tyres	£12.11s.2d	£6.5s.7d	£18.16s.9d
Michelin Whiteside tyres	£10.9s.11d	£5.5s	£15.14s.11d
Dunlop Road Speed tyres	£8.12s.6d	£4.6s.3d	£12.18s.9d

It should be noted that in some cases the prices quoted are for direct fitment by the factory in replacement for standard equipment and therefore the money value shown is merely the "extra" cost incurred. It is interesting to reflect on the lengths Jaguar went to in order to provide for every need of the 2.4 owner. For example, the bracket to raise the driver's seat – perhaps the Company had had comments from owners preferring the "sit-up-and-beg" attitude common to most luxury saloons of the day. More interesting was the availability of a factory fitted front passenger seat belt, a rarity in the mid-fifties, but no mention is made in the records of a belt suitable for the driver's seat! The reader will also note the choice of no less than ten different types of tyre and the (unusual even in the mid-fifties) listing of replacement leather panels. Disc brakes and wire wheels were still available at the same prices as quoted earlier in the chapter and the tuning modifications for the 2.4 also remained

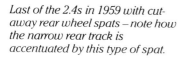

Last of the 2.4s in 1959 with cut-away rear wheel spats – note how the narrow rear track is accentuated by this type of spat.

catalogued although their popularity had decreased in favour of the 3.4 litre car.

As well as the items marked above, further accessories and options were available for the 3.4 litre models only. According to Factory records, these were only for the 3.4 although in certain cases it was feasible to have them fitted to a 2.4.

	Basic	P.Tax	Total
9 to 1 compression pistons	£36.2s.3d	£18.1s.2d	£54.3s.5d
High ratio steering box (no longer quoted for the 2.4)	£3.3s	£1.11s.6d	£4.14s.6d
Lead bronze bearings	£15.15s	£7.17s.6d	£23.12s.6d
Lightened flywheel	£1.5s	£12/6d	£1.17s.6d
Competition clutch	£7.10s	£3.15s	£11.5s
Chromium dashboard grab rail	£1.1s	10/6d	£1.11s.6d
Pyrene fire extinguisher	£3	£2.10s	£7.10s
140mph speedometer	£1.1s	10/6d	£1.11s.6d
Modified locks	£1.1s	10/6d	£1.11s.6d
Motorola Model 821 radio	£33.13s.6d	£16.16s.9d	£50.10s.3d
Master battery switch	£2.10s	£1.5s	£3.15s
Switch to cut out auto choke	£3.10s	£1.15s	£5.5s
Chromium wire wheels (5)	£77.10s	£38.15s	£116.5s
Thornton Power-Lok diff.	£30	£15	£45
Rear window demister	£4.4s	£2.2s	£6.6s
Rheostat to dashboard panel lights	£2.2s	£1.1s	£3.3s
White steering wheel (for export models only)	£1.1s	10/6d	£1.11s.6d
Gear lever extension	10/6d	5/3d	15/9d
Vanity mirror for passenger sun visor	£1.1s	10/6d	£1.11s.6d
Stiffened shock absorbers (C.14034)	£1.1s	10/6d	£1.11s.6d
Heavy duty anti-roll bar (C.14035)	£2.2s	£1.1s	£3.3s
Windtone horns	£1.1s	10/6d	£1.11s.6d

The reader will note that the majority of the above extras were ideally suited to the owner who was interested in modifying his car to competition specification, this clearly indicating the type of person at whom the 3.4 litre model was aimed. Some of the other items are interesting, for instance the modified locks, which were available simply to allow all doors, boot and glove box to be opened with the same key. The chromium dashboard grab rail was simply an idea taken from the Mark VIII model, presumably to keep the front seat passenger firmly in his seat during spirited driving! The lockable filler cap was of Desmo manufacture and was obviously an improvement over Jaguar's previous idea of taking a lock from the Mark VIII/IX.

In conclusion it cannot be over-emphasised that the 2.4 and 3.4 litre compact Jaguar saloons were an important development in the history of the Company, or that they were a tremendous success, but it must be said that nearing the end of their production run, everyone, not least Jaguar, was well aware of the models' shortcomings. The styling was by then beginning to look rather dated – even the mundane BMC Farina family saloons and the traditional Rovers, with the introduction of their 3 litre design, had much more airy, lighter interiors with quite substantial window space. The Mark I Jaguars (as we can now officially call them – Jaguar themselves taking up this term with the introduction of the Mark II range) were ripe for modification and improvement.

Three contrasting Mark Is, still surviving today in superb condition.

Total production of the 2.4 litre cars amounted to 19992 (of which over 3700 were left hand drive models) and of the 3.4 litre cars 17405 were made (approximately 8460 of which were left hand drive). From these figures it is plain to see how popular the larger engined car was in the export markets although in certain countries the 2.4 was the only model allowed (e.g. Nigeria).

During the final months of production prices remained unchanged although colour schemes were slightly amended to a choice of eleven basic colours consisting of Pearl Grey, Mist Grey, Cornish Grey, Imperial Maroon, Old English White, Indigo Blue, Cotswold Blue, Black, Sherwood Green, British Racing Green and Carmine Red. Interior trim colours at this time were red, maroon, light blue, dark blue, grey, tan or suede green. Special colour options and combinations were available to special order depending on customers' personal requirements. Some of the more unusual colour combinations requested by Mark I owners included Embassy Black with black interior and black wire wheels, Carmine Red with black interior with white piping and on one occasion an American gentleman ordered a 3.4 Mark I in Old English White with white interior and whitewall tyres with grey carpets.

With the introduction of the new Mark IIs, Mark Is were overshadowed but nevertheless remained listed alongside the new cars until September 1960 for the home market, although according to factory records the very last Mark Is left Browns Lane in September 1959; it is probable that some cars may have remained in dealers' showrooms unregistered until 1960.

The first episode in the history of the postwar compact Jaguar saloon was over; was the best still to come?

Stepping Back in Time with Mark I Jaguar

It would have been easy to fill the pages of this book with contemporary road-test material on the 2.4 and 3.4 litre Jaguars, singing the praises of the "new" cars through the eyes of the professional road-testers of the mid-fifties, all of which would have been read before in many other publications. Instead, I thought it would be much more worthwhile to look at the cars through the eyes of owners today in the hope of establishing the reasons why one might buy one of these cars, realising the advantages and disadvantages of owning and driving one in the 1980s.

Initially I needed to carry out a test and appraisal of a car in as near original condition as it was possible to get. This was necessary not only for authenticity in general but also to ensure that the vehicle behaved just as a Mark I would have behaved back in the fifties. Unfortunately a lot of cars have been restored and now do not meet the original Jaguar specifications to a lesser or greater extent, or are badly in need of work to bring them back to first-class condition. More unfortunate is the poor survival rate of the model series. Very few saloons have ever become instant classics and once the Mark II arrived on the scene the Mark I lost value and the motoring public generally lost interest.

Thankfully, I was very fortunate to be given the opportunity to drive and assess a magnificent 1956 2.4 Special Equipment model belonging to David Barnes of Sunderland. This very early car, registered on 20th September 1956 (registration number SWW220) and with chassis number 903947DN, was a manual version with overdrive and had covered a genuine 18,000 miles only from new. The car was in utterly remarkable condition, being totally original apart from the necessity of having the rear wheel spats resprayed. David is the second owner of this fine motor-car, which had resided in the north of England all its life. All the original documentation was still with the car including the M.O.T. certificates, buff coloured log book and the very first tax disc issued with the vehicle back in 1956. The car was finished in green with matching interior. SWW220 was truly a concours enthusiast's dream, beautifully preserved, and gave me an ideal opportunity to assess the model as it would have left the Jaguar factory, original, unrestored and totally unmodified.

When approaching the car, the shape and style still stood out boldly, epitomising the classic Jaguar lines of the period, and although parked next to more modern machinery, it did not look out of place or old fashioned. Upon opening the driver's door I was immediately made aware of the quality of finish, the smell of fine leather and the air of luxury from the deep pile carpeting and veneer. Jaguar were certainly correct in their comments that nothing had been spared to ensure that a 2.4 litre owner would receive the same standards of luxury as owners of the larger Mark VII. I sat in the car and closed the door with the expected quiet "clonk". On pushing the traditional Jaguar starter button the engine immediately sprang into life, emitting that clean "bark" associated with a well tuned XK engine.

During the first two to three miles of steady driving I took my time getting accustomed to the car. I immediately found the seating arrangement both firm and surprisingly comfortable, and although the 2.4 was an integrally built construction, one still sat fairly high up, on top of rather than in the driving seat. Unlike the "sit up and beg" Mark VII however, the steering wheel did not dominate the driving position and therefore allowed ample room to get in and out of the car without excessive bending and manoeuvering. There was also

plenty of leg and foot room, although I must say that my knee continually caught against the door handle. I found the steering responsive and light except when negotiating three point turns, when I have to admit the car betrayed the weight on its front wheels and the excessive number of turns from lock to lock. From the outset I found the placing of the gearlever rather awkward, necessitating a stretch for the left arm in order to engage first, third and reverse gears. After a while at the wheel this got decidedly annoying and I tended to engage second gear at give-way junctions to avoid the long stretch into first. Having said that, during normal driving the gearbox behaved well and was usually smooth in operation, except when changing from third to second when I found it best to double de-clutch. At odd times first gear was also difficult to engage, a common failure with the old Moss gearbox where first does not have synchromesh fitted. First gear also had the expected whine common to all these gearboxes but in all other respects the transmission was excellent. Laycock de Normanville overdrive was fitted to this car and although it operated perfectly, I found the positioning of the switch on the far right top of the dashboard awkward to use, although I have seen other 2.4s with the switch positioned further down the dashboard which must make matters even worse.

On conventional road surfaces the 2.4 was quiet and comfortable, and despite the relatively small window area it did not seem at all claustrophobic. On the open motorway the car accelerated well through the gears with no sign of fussiness and I found little advantage in pressing the engine beyond 4,000 rpm in any gear. The car became particularly smooth and accelerated well between 60 and 80mph at which time engaging overdrive reduced the revs and noise level considerably. Accelerating beyond 80mph betrayed the small engine size and the 2.4 lacked that extra urge. The car suffered from a minor wheel vibration above 60mph but nevertheless was remarkably stable and smooth at 90mph and over. Wind noise presented no real problem despite the fact that the rubber door seals must have weakened over the years.

On winding country lanes the 2.4 behaved predictably, coping superbly with uneven road conditions and showing no sign of scuttle shake, rattles or other irritations, thus emphasising the sound engineering in Jaguar's first attempt at unitary construction. The whole body seemed exceptionally taut and solid. I can honestly confess that this car felt stronger than any other comparable sized car I have driven. Although best suited to fast driving on open straight roads in overdrive top, the 2.4 was also at home on the twisting country lanes around Sunderland and it was easy to see why the model was so popular with competitive drivers in the late fifties and early sixties. I did, however, find that on hills constant gear changing was necessary to maintain adequate acceleration and this was the one area where the small 2.4 litre engine was at its worst, although the engine did not seem to lack the torque for quite good getaways from road junctions in second gear.

The most disappointing aspect of the 2.4 to me lay in the brakes, or should I have said the lack of them! Probably in 1956 they did not appear to be that bad in the light of brake technology of the time, when everyday family saloons and even luxury class status symbols could not maintain speeds in excess of 100mph, but by today's standards when even the most mundane cars have disc brakes, the 2.4 lost points in my assessment. Even though the drum brakes were power assisted, I found it easy to overestimate the stopping power of the car; even when decelerating from quite modest speeds extra foresight was necessary and reasonably heavy pressure on the brake pedal. On country lanes approaching bends and declines care was needed, although the more miles I drove the more confident I became, but on the assumption that the majority of people who would buy a car like this today would do so as a second vehicle, it would be very easy to forget how poor the brakes were in comparison to the everyday Ford! I had no reason to assume that the brakes on this 2.4 were inferior to those on any other Mark Is and indeed they were comparable to other drum braked cars I had driven, but nevertheless they were not up to the performance of the car, a conclusion also drawn by Jaguar themselves on the introduction of the 3.4 litre version.

As for the interior, legroom for both front and rear passengers was adequate, more than one would normally expect from a car of such compact dimensions in the fifties. Minor irritations with the interior included the placing of the small indicator stalk, which did not fall easily to the right hand, and the green indicator tell-tale (just off the steering column situated on the indicator stalk boss) was hardly visible due to the positioning of the steering wheel spokes. There was also no audible indicator "tick" to help matters. The standard convex rear-view mirror was not a lot of help in combination with the small rear window. David had found the same problem and had therefore fitted a clip-over larger diameter flat-glass type. Some of the dashboard controls were obviously better suited to left-hand drive cars, for example the wiper switch on the far left-hand side of the dashboard was very awkward to reach from the driver's seat. I also thought it unfortunate that a car of this standard was not equipped with a separate interior light for the front seat passenger, a very useful aid on other Jaguar models for map reading, etc. The instruments were very clear to read and seemed precise in operation and the 5″ diameter speedometer and rev. counter had very period arrow-heads attached to the indicator needles. The fresh-air heater worked remarkably well, better in fact than in many compact Jaguars I have known – unusual to say the least! The handbrake was situated easily to hand and worked efficiently, negating another frequent complaint from Jaguar owners. The pedals were well positioned and the bucket front seats were easily adjustable for any size of driver.

In conclusion the 2.4 was a dream to drive despite the lack of an efficient braking system and the long stretch of the gear lever. I thought the car an excellent and underrated classic. Although I appreciate this can be said of many quality cars of the fifties, it must be difficult for anyone to realise how good the 2.4 Mark I is without actually driving one. It is certainly a driver's car, a rare sight on or off the road today, and would provide its owner with many miles of very enjoyable classic motoring.

I next chose to look at the Mark I through the eyes of a present day owner who regularly used his car come rain , snow or sunshine. I consulted a man who not only used his car as everyday transport but at the same time appreciated the fine engineering and wished to preserve his Mark I in tip-top condition. Whilst it would be unfair of me to criticise the concours brigade (in fact they do an excellent job in presserving classic cars) they do not, in the majority of cases, use their cars to the full and perhaps are not totally aware of all the idiosyncracies or benefits of owning such a car and using it as originally intended.

I therefore contacted Jack Smith, who is in the R.A.F. based in North Yorkshire. Jack's car was a 1958 2.4 litre Special Equipment model, registration number 1222DT, chassis number 910398, painted in British Racing Green with tan interior trim. The car was a manual model and although not supplied from new with overdrive, had had this option fitted in 1964 by a previous owner. Registered on the 12th April 1958, the car had had two previous careful owners who both resided in the Yorkshire area. The car now has a genuine speedometer reading of about 80,000 miles of which Jack Smith had put on over 30,000 miles himself in a little over a year's ownership. The car is remarkably original, in excellent order and apart from a bottom half respray a few years ago has had no major work carried out.

I met Jack at the R.A.F. base one very cold and wet Sunday morning and we immediately set off for a warm-up run in the Yorkshire countryside, at which time we discussed his car in detail. Jack likes to use his car and thinks that these fine Jaguars were meant to be used to the full rather than cosseted for dry, sunny days only. He frequently uses his Mark I to commute northwards from Yorkshire to Scotland, visiting friends and relations, and he assured me that on these long runs the 2.4 had little trouble maintaining 28mpg in overdrive top, quite comparable with modern day "tin cans" as Jack put it.

Jack first saw the car advertised in a local garage and was quite surprised that a classic Mark I Jaguar could still be found at an affordable price in such remarkably good condition. He had never previously owned a Jaguar, let alone a Mark I, but had always admired the 2.4 and 3.4 cars for their period looks and good design. Upon purchasing the car he was pleasantly surprised at the responsiveness of the 2.4 litre engine despite many remarks from people that the smaller engined Jaguar was a poor performer. He was also encouraged by the solidity of the car on bad road surfaces, the general finish and the high degree of comfort from a 25 year old car. In Jack's own words, "the car in appearance and performance was far better than I could have expected." His only criticism of the performance aspect concerned the car's "pullability" at certain revs, when the engine lost out to many other cars with more torque. Jack also found the long travel of the gear lever from first to second an annoyance , and the lack of synchromesh on first gear proved a problem when rolling up to road junctions.

During our Sunday morning drive, it was clear that Jack knew his car well, and he had no trouble maintaining a high average speed around the twisting Yorkshire country lanes, using the gears to keep up his average speed. The car cornered exceptionally well on standard tyres in spite of the wet and very windy conditions. Despite a slight leak from an exhaust flexi-pipe the Mark I was very quiet and even when driven hard did not sound rough or uneasy.

Jack Smith's 2.4.

Jack likes the steering, explaining that it is light yet responsive on the move. His Mark I had a sporting feel which encouraged spirited driving.

Jack's 2.4 is fitted with the standard drum brakes but he maintains that they are not too bad in operation, especially once you get used to them. He obviously knows the brakes' limitations and although he drives the car hard is careful and respectful enough to realise the maximum efficiency he can expect from the system.

Concerning the interior, Jack has found the seating arrangement particularly comfortable, which again encourages sporting driving as the bucket-type front seats do not allow the driver to slide around, even without seat belts. He commented that the gauges were very plain and easy to read and that the heater was adequate although no more than that. Jack gets rather annoyed at the continual problem of misting up as he finds the demister very inefficient. The rear window particularly was a constant source of trouble on our journey so Jack is contemplating the fitment of a heated rear window panel to alleviate the problem.

Jack Smith intends keeping his 2.4 Mark I and is keen to ensure that the car stays in its present condition. He is confident that it is possible to use a car like this yet at the same time keep it in a healthy state of repair by protecting it against the elements to ensure survival of the original body panels. Of course he is aware of the possibility of an accident causing severe damage to difficult-to-replace body panels but he feels the car is such a joy to drive that this is worth the risk. Jack Smith is convinced that the Mark I saloon is a very practical classic car and is still excellent value for money.

The Mark I Jaguar in Competition

The peak period of Jaguar's involvement in racing, rallying and other forms of competitive sport was the fifties and early sixties. This period saw the great Le Mans successes for the C Types and D Types and the many rally victories for the Mark VII and XKs. The introduction of the 2.4 litre saloon provided a formidable weapon for Jaguar on the race circuits and rally routes. The new compact saloon proved an excellent successor to the much larger Mark VIIs and was, in many ways, comparable to the XKs. Mark Is were undoubtedly more flexibly sprung than the Mark VIIs and the compact dimensions were to prove a distinct advantage on rallies.

The 2.4 made its competition debut in the 1956 RAC Rally. 162 cars out of an initial 205 finished the rally and despite stiff competition from Aston Martin, Morgan, and Jaguar's own XK140 (handled by the top class Appleyard team), a 2.4 (registration number JWK753) took a very creditable 4th place overall, driven by W.D. Bleakley and I.J. Hall. This same car and team took first place in the over 2,000cc class, beating Ian Appleyard, who took third place in his XK. To quote *Autocar* of 16th March 1956, "The 2.4 looked right, sounded very healthy and the only complaints one heard were of unnecessarily low geared steering and a touch of brake fade in a tight section" – comments levelled at Jaguars many times.

In the Great American Mountain Rally of 1956, the 2.4 also made a name for itself by finishing first in the 1,500 to 3,000cc Touring Class. Despite freezing conditions, as low as 17° below zero, plenty of snow, ice and navigational problems, the 2.4 did exceptionally well.

On to racing for 1956, and the race to put the compact Jaguars on the map was the Spa Production Car Race in Belgium, in which Paul Frère in a factory prepared 2.4 won the 10 lap touring car race at over 90mph in May.

A 2.4 competing in the MGCC Brands Hatch meeting on 29th September 1957.

This gave the Mark I its first outright victory. The car concerned had a "C" type head, 2" S.U. carburettors and a close-ratio gearbox. Frère also won his class and managed the best performance of any car in any class.

Also in May of 1956 Jaguar prepared a team of 2.4s to compete in the Production Car Race at Silverstone. The cars were prepared for Mike Hawthorn and Duncan Hamilton. Hawthorn initially took the lead but had to drop out with a broken valve after only two laps. Hamilton went on to finish in third place having held that position since the fifth lap.

It was at this time that Jaguar announced their official retirement from the competition scene and although no more works cars were to be available, Jaguar still prepared cars for private owners and offered advice whenever possible.

1957 proved a memorable year for Jaguars, memorable for good and bad reasons. The factory fire on 12th February could have put paid to Jaguar's future but the good news was that year the 2.4s and 3.4s swept all before them on the competition scene. In The Silverstone Production Car Race of that year (held in September) the new 3.4 litre saloons showed their paces. 3.4s were prepared by the factory for Duncan Hamilton, Mike Hawthorn and Ivor Bueb. These three cars were quite extensively modified, with heavy duty anti-roll bars front and rear, competition rear shock absorbers, extra leaves to the rear springs and Power-Lok limited slip differentials. The engines were equipped with "C" type cylinder heads, high lift camshafts, twin 2" S.U. carburettors, 9 to 1 compression pistons and lead bronze bearings. A racing clutch was fitted along with a close-ratio gearbox with overdrive locked out. The rear axle ratio was uprated to 3.5 and the battery was transferred to the boot for better weight distribution. Racing tyres were also fitted and last but not least a straight-through exhaust system was substituted. To quote the *Autosport* magazine of the period, "my word how they go" was no understatement!

The three Jaguars were hurled around the bends for all they were worth,

A 2.4 competing in the London Rally on 21st September 1956.

apparently with the door handles nearly scraping the ground. The whole process was quite horrifying. For five laps Mike Hawthorn was followed by Archie Scott-Brown in another 3.4 with Duncan Hamilton and Ivor Bueb wheel to wheel behind. Soon after, Scott-Brown had to retire through brake fade problems (drum brakes) leaving Mike Hawthorn with an unassailable lead. A 2.4 litre saloon was also entered by Ron Flockhart, prepared by the John Coombs organisation, and although this appeared to be much steadier than the 3.4s, it was nowhere near as quick. Mike Hawthorn went on to win the race in his 3.4 (registered RVC592) at an average speed of 82.19mph, breaking the previous year's lap record held by a Mark VII at 81.68mph. Second place went to Duncan Hamilton at an average of 81.73mph and third place man was Ivor Bueb at an average of 80.11mph. Ron Flockhart in the 2.4 litre car (TBM2) finished a very creditable 5th at an average of over 76mph. Needless to say the team prize also went to Jaguar, marking the true beginning of their dominance in saloon car competition for the next few years.

At the Christmas Brands Hatch Touring Car Race held on Boxing Day of 1957 Tommy Sopwith got out in front from the start in a 3.4, driving as if the devil were behind him and producing smoke from the tyres on each and every corner. An astounding duel developed behind him between Sir Gawaine Baillie in another 3.4 and a Ford Anglia. On the straight Baillie's Jaguar had the speed but the Anglia easily beat him around the bends. The race was won by Sopwith for Jaguar at an average speed of 61.61mph with Baillie managing 2nd place. Sopwith also took the fastest lap, at 63.77mph, which became a new saloon car record.

On the Rally scene in 1957 three 3.4s competed in the touring car category of the Tour de France. The lead was initially held by two of the Jaguars, driven by Da Silva Ramos/Monnoyeur and Consten/Renel, but both cars unfortunately had to retire before the end of the race. The third 3.4 driven by Sir Gawaine Baillie and Peter Jopp could also have done well but burst a

Frank Ward in his 3.4 taking part in a JDC rally in Derbyshire in the late fifties.

tyre, leaving the road and finally catching fire. In the 1957 Tulip Rally the Morley brothers put up a creditable effort in their newly acquired 2.4 litre saloon, taking third place in their class.

1958 proved to be another successful year for the Mark Is. In the Monte Carlo Rally no less than thirty Jaguars were entered, most of which were 3.4s. First away from the Glasgow starting point was the 3.4 (VRW34) of Frank Watts. The Athens starting point was chosen by the Monégasque Jaguar entry of Carris and Beziers, who finished 24th overall and second in their class and were the best placed Jaguar in the whole rally. Other 3.4 entries included Peter Jopp, Brown, Arnold, and Eric Brinkman, who nearly rolled his car on more than one occasion. Jaguars again proved their worth in the RAC Rally. On the first test stage at Prescott, Sopwith was fastest in his class with a 3.4 and at the end of the rally Waddilove won his class in a 2.4, with Brinkman first in his class with a 3.4, followed by Sopwith in second place. In the Tour De France (touring car category) Jaguar had the Whitehead brothers, Tommy Sopwith and Sir Gawaine Baillie with Peter Jopp, all driving 3.4s. With such experienced drivers Jaguar stood an excellent chance of winning this section. Sopwith drove magnificently and soon took the lead in his class with the Whitehead brothers close behind. Unfortunately Jaguar suffered a terrible loss when, whilst entering Le Touquet, Sopwith's car collided with a taxi and, to quote the *Autocar* report of 3rd October, "Sopwith explained that he was a bit pressed, but the taxi driver complained that his car was a bit squashed and insisted on waiting for a policeman." Very inconsiderate! The delay put Sopwith out of the rally. Peter Whitehead then took the lead but unfortunately due to carburation trouble dropped position later on. Although regaining their lead again, the Whiteheads had a fatal accident when their car took a corner, ran off the road and fell some 30 feet. Graham Whitehead was driving at this time and although he was only slightly hurt, his brother Peter died from injuries. The one remaining Mark I, driven by Sir Gawaine Baillie and Peter Jopp, went on to finish third in class. To quote *Autocar* again, "In series production touring cars, however, we have in the Jaguar 3.4 a car which is capable of winning this type of event in spite of its weight handicap. If it had not been for the minor accident at Le Touquet and the major accident in the Cevennes, either Sopwith or the Whiteheads could have brought a British car into first place in this category, and what could have been done this year, can be done next; let us hope it will be."

Geoff Uren's 3.4 in the Silverstone paddock shortly after losing a wheel.

Roy Salvadori cornering well at the Silverstone British Grand Prix saloon car race on 19th July 1958.

In the 1958 Tulip Rally (reputedly the toughest up till that time) the Morley brothers from East Anglia entered their 2.4 (DJM400) along with Frank Grounds/Laurie Hands in another 2.4 and Ernie Haddan, who had to retire early due to sheared brake caliper bolts. Other entries included R.H. Wilkin and J. Alexandre in a 3.4 (EYK417), Parkes and Cuff in a 3.4 (DKV450) and Ian Appleyard and W. Bleakley in another 3.4. After only 36 hours of hard driving a mere 25 competitors were left unpenalised, including the Morley brothers, but at the end only three cars had been able to amass the maximum number of 145 points, one of which was Parkes in his 3.4, Volvo and Saab being the other two. Appleyard dropped out earlier with exhaust trouble but the Morleys put up a fantastic performance, winning the F Touring Cars (2,000/2,600cc) class and becoming the best placed British participants with a very creditable 8th place overall. Brinkman took 32nd overall in another Mark I (also receiving 2nd in the 2,600cc and over class). Frank Grounds managed 79th place in his 2.4. In the Acropolis Rally of that year a 2.4 came second driven by a Greek team. In the RSAC Scottish Rally a 3.4 driven by Parkes took first place in its class and in the Liège-Rome-Liège Rally another success was recorded for Jaguar with a win by Lindner and Walters in a 3.4 Mark I.

On the race circuits in 1958 things looked just as good for Jaguar and the Mark I. At the Touring Car Race at Silverstone 32 cars commenced from a Le Mans type start. The Jaguar successes were continued in a spectacular manner with a race-long battle between Mike Hawthorn in a 3.4 (VDU881) and Tommy Sopwith in his 3.4 (EN400). Other Mark Is were entered by Sir Gawaine Baillie, Ivor Bueb and Ron Flockhart. Sopwith made a lightning getaway from the start but Hawthorn soon caught him up on the 5th lap and passed, establishing a precarious lead. The two cars often travelled side by side down the straights, battling for position. They were followed by Ron Flockhart in his John Coombs modified car and this trio were well ahead of the rest of the field by all of 20 laps — it must have been a tremendous sight. The final outcome was Duncan Hamilton first at 84.22mph (only 0.8 seconds faster than the second man), Sopwith taking second place with Flockhart third. Mike Hawthorn made the fastest lap of the day in 2 minutes 1 second at a speed of 87.08mph.

51

A special saloon car race was held on the grand prix day at Silverstone during that year. Baillie, Sopwith and Hansgen competed and Sir William Lyons himself was in attendance. Tommy Sopwith had produced the fastest time in practice (85.95mph). Walter Hansgen was the then current sports car champion of the U.S.A. and competed at this event in a maroon (John Coombs prepared) 3.4, the only Mark I on the day with steel wheels as opposed to the now established wires. In practice Hansgen was only fractionally slower than Tommy Sopwith. For the first ten laps of the race's seventeen these two fought it out well ahead of all the opposition, Hansgen's cornering technique of deliberately "losing" the Jaguar's tail and putting the front wheels on opposite lock seeming to drop him little time, while greatly thrilling the appreciative spectators. On lap 6 Sopwith had to mow the grass opposite the pits when trying to overtake an assortment of other cars and then, five laps later, his car shed a rear wheel (slightly injuring a spectator) at Becketts and the American advanced into an unchallenged lead to the finish. Hansgen won the race in his 3.4 (TWK287) at an average speed of 83.92mph. Sir Gawaine Baillie came second, Crawley third and Uren fourth, all in 3.4s, with the fastest lap of the race put up by Sopwith at 86.09mph.

In October at the Brands Hatch meeting Sopwith this time managed to pull the winning stroke in his 3.4, repeating the performance in the One Hour Race for GT and Special Series Saloons at Snetterton on the 11th October. At the start of this race Sopwith quickly moved up to first place in his dark blue car, and not long after this Sir Gawaine Baillie in another 3.4 dropped out of the race with rear axle trouble. Another Mark I competitor was Peter Jopp in a 2.4. *Autocar* in its race report of 17th October commented, "Sopwith's Jaguar – sounding magnificent as it tore up the main straight – continued in the lead to win at 78.85mph."

In the saloon car race at Crystal Palace during the BRSCC meeting (the first time saloon cars had raced at the event) Sopwith was first yet again in his 3.4 at 66.88mph with Baillie coming second and Uren third, both also in 3.4s. Sopwith also took the fastest lap at 67.8mph.

For 1959 the winning reputation of the Mark I saloons was upheld. At the Silverstone Production Car Race, out of a field of 26 starters, Jaguar continued their unbroken record of eleven consecutive annual wins at the event. To say that the small Jaguar saloons stole the show is a massive understatement. Ivor Bueb (who was at that time team leader for Equipe Endeavour) won the race in his 3.4, taking the lap record to 88.6mph, followed by other 3.4s taking second (Salvadori in a Coombs modified car registered 287 JPK), third (Sir Gawaine Baillie in UXD400), fourth (Protheroe), and fifth (Dickson), not forgetting Peter Bland taking sixth place in a 2.4! The FIRST SIX places went to Jaguar and the now legendary Mark I. Ivor Bueb took first place again in the saloon car scratch race at Aintree in the same year with his 3.4 (IVA400) at an average of 74.99mph, with Roy Salvadori second in another 3.4 (287JPK) and Sir Gawaine Baillie third, again in a 3.4. On this occasion the fastest lap went to Salvadori at 76.70mph. Peter Bland took second place in his class with a 2.4. Ivor led throughout the race with Roy Salvadori hot on his heels. The position of the first four cars never altered and a magnificent spectacle was provided by the two 3.4 litre Jaguars cornering at impossible speeds with smoke pouring from the back tyres. Ivor not only won the race but broke Sopwith's old record (unofficially) by one second and bettered the old lap record by some 2½mph. At the spring Goodwood meeting in the saloon car scratch race, the dynamic trio of Bueb, Salvadori and Baillie did it again, taking first, second and third places respectively. Ivor Bueb drove the Equipe Endeavour 3.4 (IVA400), with Roy Salvadori in a John Coombs car. Bueb lapped incidentally at 78.40mph. To close on circuit racing for 1959 Walter Hansgen won the 1959 U.S.A. grand prix compact saloon car race in a works prepared 3.4.

Moving on to the rally scene for 1959, Bobby Parkes and Arthur Senior competed in the Alpine Rally, only to lose out after exceeding the speed limits

The Don and Erle Morley 3.4 winning the 1959 Tulip Rally.

in their 3.4 (OKY450). In the Monte Carlo Rally of that year Bobby Parkes competed with Howarth in the same privately entered car and won the group 1 touring class. Other 3.4s of Walton/Martin, Brinkman/Cuff and Cooper/Barker also participated and all achieved good results, enabling Jaguar to take the Charles Faroux Award for the best result from a one-make team. Parkes took 8th place with Walton in 9th, Brinkman in 37th and Cooper in 56th place.

Appalling weather conditions affected the 1959 R.A.C. Rally, in which a 3.4 Mark I was entered by Bobby Parkes and a 2.4 litre model by Viscount Boyne. The Parkes car finished well down the field but the car of Boyne (and Brassey) finished 50th overall. In the Tour de France Graham Whitehead ran a 3.4 and was lying a comfortable second when he had to retire after a collision. This left the field open to Da Silva Ramos who eventually won in another 3.4. For the 11th International Tulip Rally of that year, reputed to be the worst to date because of very severe weather conditions, the Morley brothers drove to outright victory in their new and privately entered 3.4 (again registered DJM400). In the Scottish Rally of that year a 2.4 (AC43) driven by Gerry Flewitt won its class and in the rather obscure 1959 Sestrisie Rally Plant and Heinemann came second in the over 1,600cc touring class with their 3.4 (registered HP312). Unfortunately in the Coronation Safari Rally Jaguar received no honours despite a brave try by Lloyd and Walker in a 2.4 (registered KFK842).

J.B.Scott passes Newark Priory in his 3.4 during the first day's run from Ascot to Edinburgh in the 1959 Mobilgas Economy Run. The 3.4 managed a very creditable 34.2mpg.

On a different aspect of competition, a 3.4 litre Mark I driven by J.B. Scott (34EPC) averaged 34.20mpg in the British Mobilgas Economy Run in 1959, although this figure was beaten the previous year in the Rhodesian Mobilgas Economy Run by another 3.4 (B37841) averaging a very thrifty 35.59mpg.

Before closing the page on yet another very successful year for the compact Jaguars, it should not be forgotten that Mike Hawthorn tragically lost his life in that year whilst driving his personal 3.4 Mark I on the Guildford bypass on the 22nd January. Apparently the car was struck by a strong gust of wind and was blown across the road, inducing a skid which he was unable to control. The car struck the back of an oncoming lorry and then hit a tree, breaking in two. Hawthorn suffered a fractured skull and died almost instantly; a tragic loss, not only to Jaguar, but to the whole world of competitive motoring.

1960 saw the Mark II saloons take to the competition scene carrying the flag for Jaguar. In certain cases the Mark Is managed to soldier on. In the Lyons Charbonnières Rally of March that year, Gentilini and Justanord won their class in a 3.4 and managed third in the general classification. In the Monte Carlo Rally the 3.4s of Walter and Pinder failed to finish, unfortunately defeated by fuel problems. Mark Is continued to participate in minor rallies and other events throughout 1960 and 61, the last effective Mark I result being first place in class in the 1961 Circuit of Ireland race, the car a 3.4 driven by H.J. O'Connor-Rorke and J. Cuff.

During the period 1956 to 1960 Mark Is were popular not only with

A 2.4 competing in a hill-climb in Belfast around 1961.

A Mark I going for a spin in a JDC inter-area challenge race in 1983.

owners and drivers but also with the thousands of spectators who loved the spectacle of these fine race-bred cars. In the ensuing years Mark Is were relegated to more minor and unglamorous aspects of competition in the form of grass-track and even banger racing. Mark Is did continue with some success in Club events and a revival of interest was to take place in the early

Mark Is at speed at a club meeting in 1982.

seventies with the onset of classic saloon car racing and in particular the Pre '57 Saloon Car Championships. For this championship Mark Is had to have bodies as near as possible to original specification with no "luxury" extras like limited slip differentials, etc. On the track alongside the Ford Zephyrs, Austin A30s and the like, the old Jaguars still look completely at home.

Other Mark Is thrived in the seventies like UXF 363, the very successful Albert Betts modified car with 3.8 litre engine. Roger Andreason also handled a modified Mark I (7 KMD) with terrific success. This 2.4 litre car amassed no fewer than four wins at Mallory Park, two at Lydden Hill, two at Castle Combe, two wins and one third place at Silverstone, two wins and one second placing at Brands Hatch, and wins at Thruxton, Cadwell Park, Donington and Snetterton.

Such successes encouraged the Mark I and II Register of the Jaguar Drivers' Club to instigate their Inter-Area Challenge Race Series (more of which in a later chapter). The current revival in classic car competition enables us all to enjoy the sight and sound of the great Mark I Jaguars in action again.

Grass-track racing, the ignominious end for many Mark Is.

Evolution of the Mark II

1959 was to become a memorable year, not only for Jaguar but for the whole motoring world. At that time more cars were being purchased than ever before and in fact one in every three families owned a motor vehicle. Petrol cost just under five shillings per gallon, which to many was still extortionate, and Britain's first motorway, the M1, had just opened. 1959 saw the introduction of several interesting and important new models, among them the Mini, unorthodox and yet the most important small car of the decade. There was also the Triumph Herald, pioneering bolt-on body panels and giving rise to a variety of small cars based on the same mechanical theme. New models in the sports car field included the Daimler SP250 with its unusual styling and extensive use of glass fibre ,and at the top end of the market place there was the Aston Martin DB4, epitomising the very best in British quality car manufacture.

At this time Jaguar profits were exceeding one million pounds per year and their cars were selling well. Despite this, the Company did not sit back. Even though the 2.4 and 3.4 Mark Is were very successful and popular (in fact outselling the larger Jaguar saloons by some four to one), Jaguar realised that their compact saloons were being critisised by many for their unpredictable handling and outdated appearance. Jaguar had in fact been working on a completely revamped car, and they launched their "new" Mark II in October 1959, coinciding with the Motor Show at Earls Court. I refer here to the Mark II range as "new" because it is hard to visualise greater improvements being

Mark II bodyshell awaiting paint at the factory.

made to the existing Mark I without undertaking an entirely new body design. The Mark IIs were very different, not just in appearance but also in character, and brought the compact Jaguar well and truly into the 60s. The Mark II was all things to all men – an ideal car for the family man who required quality, comfort and style, or for the businessman who needed the prestige of a quality British saloon, or even for the man about town who had dispensed with his sports car.

The prices asked for the Mark II cars (starting at £1,082) made other quality cars seem decidedly expensive in comparison, especially when taking into consideration the specification of the new small Jaguar. The practice of maintaining economies of manufacture by utilising as many parts from existing models as possible was an important factor in keeping the prices down and yet maintaining the quality. This and long-term production with little change to the basic concept ensured superb value for money throughout the production life of the car.

There were very few cars in direct competition with the Mark II. The Humber Super Snipe was of a similar size and was slightly quicker than the 2.4 litre Jaguar but it was no match for the 3.4 or 3.8, and it did not possess the style or mechanical excellence of the Jaguar. The Rover 3 litre could also have been considered a competitor to the small Jaguar although built for a different market. The new Mark IIs also captured buyers from a much wider field; the 2.4 litre models became one step up for the usual purchasers of Austin Westminsters, Ford Zodiacs, Vauxhall Crestas and the like, the Jaguar being cheap to buy and insure. The 3.8 litre version became very popular with more sporting motorists and here gained a lot of buyers from the traditional sports car market; car makers like AC, Austin Healey and MG all lost customers to the 3.8 Jaguar as did many of the more upmarket manufacturers like Bristol and Aston Martin.

In the Mark II, Jaguar corrected most of the criticisms levelled against the previous models, ensuring that the new range would become one of the most successful Jaguars to date, sales only being surpassed by the XJ6 Series. The Mark IIs were firm favourites not only with the everyday motorist but also with competition drivers. With the Mark II, Jaguar were also out to attack export saloon car markets as never before, the 3.8 model being more than a match for any American competition. Indeed the model notched up a couple of Best Imported Car Awards in the U.S.A; and to further Jaguar's penetration into other export areas, they even set up assembly plants in countries like South Africa. In this way they got round restrictive import regulations which had previously only allowed Jaguar to import the very basic 2.4 litre models.

Now let us look at the many alterations, modifications and improvements made by Jaguar to their compact saloon car range in 1959. We will begin by examining the exterior of the Mark II. Here most of the overall styling from the Mark I was retained, and in fact nearly all the internal body panels are common to both cars; this aspect alone is a credit to Sir William Lyons' ability to design cars utilising existing tooling to keep production costs down. Most of the exterior panels, however, were substantially altered, with the exception of the bonnet, sills and boot lid. Looking from the front of the car and identifying the various changes, firstly the radiator grille was altered and now included a thick chromium rib running down the centre and effectively splitting the grille in half. It retained the engine size badge at the top of the grille, although in a more prominent fashion. The traditional Jaguar horn grilles flanking the radiator grille on the left and right were also changed to a neater style with quite distinctive curvature. Although this feature was retained on all export models during production, very shortly after commencement of manufacture U.K. cars had these grilles replaced by flush-fitting Lucas Fogranger lamps until the onset of the 240/340 when the grilles returned again. The front wings were also modified and now included bezels set into the top of the wings for the sidelights, which had a small red tell-tale on the uppermost edge informing the driver that the bulbs were working when the

Mark I meets Mark II. Note the extra glass area of the Mark II design.

lights were switched on. The positioning of the sidelights in this manner was normal Jaguar practice at the time and had been a feature of all models going back to the pre-war SS days. The same applied to the revised positioning of the front indicator lights, now fitted to the lower half of the front wing curvature.

The biggest improvements over the original Mark I body design were made in the centre, passenger section, with dramatically increased glass areas (some 9½" of extra glass width per side). The windscreen was much deeper, making it a full 16½" of glass, and was now more curved with an extra inch taken off the windscreen pillars and B (central door pillar) post. Normal toughened glass was used as previously, although a laminated screen was available for an extra cost of £7.8s.6d. The doors were substantially altered and gone were the full door frames with enormously thick window surrounds. Instead the doors now terminated at waist level and chromium window frames were bolted on to the door sections – another instance where Jaguar reverted to the policy used on other models going back to the Mark V. The front door windows were now 1¼" deeper and the quarterlights were also modified to provide a spring-held opening at 40° with a further two "notched" opening positions allowing extra ventilation as required. Centrally placed catches were used for the quarterlights in the belief that these were more thief-

Frontal aspects of the two models. Note the larger screen of the Mark II and the overriders placed further apart.

Rear ends. Note differing rear lights and badging and the pronounced difference in rear screen size.

proof; in practice this type of catch was just as easily sprung open. On the B post a chromium finisher was used, matching the window frames. Rear door windows were also much deeper and they too had enlarged quarterlights (with elaborate swivel catches allowing a maximum opening of approximately 4″), as previously used on Jaguar saloons back to the Mark V and even at one time by Rolls Royce. Chromium rain gutters were now evident along with new slim door handles designed to keep the locks free from dirt and dust. Chrome beading was fitted to the top edge of all doors giving a little extra finish to the sides of the car and complementing a chromium waistline trim which ran from the leading edge of the bonnet to meet the rear bumper as on the previous Mark I. The rear window was now of much larger dimensions, 3″ deeper and 7″ wider, of a semi-wraparound type almost meeting the rear door quarterlights. The whole effect of these changes amounted to a much lighter interior, making the car seem substantially bigger inside. *Autocar* commented that the car had "unrestricted visibility" – which must have been the first time such a comment was made about a Jaguar saloon!

At the rear of the car the general shape of the body remained unchanged although the rear wings were modified to accept the wider track of the new axle and the rear valance was enlarged below the bumper to fully conceal the fuel tank. The rear bumper was also altered, being very slightly wider, and now embodied a "Disc Brake" badge fitted in the middle directly in line with the boot lock. The rear light clusters were enlarged, now employing a separate lens and bulb for the indicators and a much larger chromium (Mazak based) surround. The new lights were very similar to those fitted to later Mark IXs and XK 150s although they were not interchangeable. Badging on the boot lid now included a discreet "Mk II" in the bottom right-hand corner.

Cutaway wheel spats were retained over the rear wheels similar to those used on the Mark I, although of very slightly smaller dimensions, the depth of the spat at its centre being slightly under 6″ whereas the Mark I's were exactly 6″, and the lipped rear edge was slightly less pronounced. (In Jaguar's records there seems to be no apparent reason for this slight alteration unless it was due to a change of supplier). The wheels of the Mark II were as fitted to the earlier cars, 15″, and painted to match body colour, with traditional Jaguar hub-caps. Wheel trims were still considered an extra, available either as the chromium Rimbellisher type or the fully enclosed Ace Turbo style, replacing

the hub-caps entirely. As before, wire wheels in body colour, chromium or stove enamel finish were available as an extra, nearly always fitted to export cars along with whitewall tyres.

Looking now at the interior of the new car, the only items remaining unchanged from the Mark I were the door and window handles and the rear seat cushion. All the other equipment and fittings were totally new, bringing the car up to date in terms of refinement. The seats had leather facings as usual for a Jaguar, the individual front seats being much larger and thicker than previously although less shapely in the backs. Set into the backs of these seats were small wood-veneered picnic tables for use by rear seat passengers. The rear seat back, although of the same shaping as the Mark I, was now made from one piece of leather whereas previously two separate pieces were used, being visibly stitched in the top centre. The interior was fully carpeted in best quality Wilton of a different weave from that used previously, and entirely new to a saloon Jaguar was a console running down from the centre of the dashboard between the front seats, trimmed in good quality textured nylon. This console housed the radio (usually an HMV or Motorola), a chromium rectangular speaker grille flanked by the heater and demister slide controls, and beneath these a large rectangular ashtray with a hinged flip-up lid, again trimmed to match, with a Jaguar head set into the lid top. Further back on the console between the seats was the gearlever with leather boot. Inside the console two flexible heater pipes ducted warm air from the heater to the rear compartment, terminating in a chromium grille angled towards the floor on

either side. The heater itself, incidentally, had an increased output of 3.9 kilowatts, although it must be said that the system was still very inadequate even by the standards of the day and was a constant source of complaint from owners.

The interior door panels (again finished in imitation leather to keep costs down) had large spring-loaded map pockets to the front with wider rigid pockets in the rear doors. All four doors had armrests and the rear ones had inset ashtrays with slide-open lids. Veneered door cappings were fitted to all doors with veneer finishing to the central door pillars. Inset into the roof lining were no fewer than four interior lights connected to courtesy switches on all doors and also to a toggle switch on the dashboard. Twin sunvisors were inset into the headlining (*á la* Mark IX) although this type was later modified to a more conventional swivel type. The driver's rear view mirror was now bolted to the roof directly between the visors on all cars, a practice adopted on some late production Mark Is. The layout of the dashboard was on an entirely new theme, a theme which was to be followed on all subsequent models (both saloon and sports) right up to the Series II XJ. Wood veneer was of course extensively used. The speedometer and rev. counter were now sited directly in front of the driver, the rev. counter incorporating an integral electric clock and the speedometer having tell-tale lights for low fuel level and ignition warning as well as total mileage and trip odometer. To the right hand side of the two main instruments (right hand drive cars), there was a large red warning light wired up to the handbrake so that it lit up whenever the handbrake was in the "on" position. This light was also wired to a simple float mechanism in the brake fluid reservoir and would consequently also light up when the fluid level was low. The remaining space on this side of the dashboard was utilised for the manual choke slider control on 2.4 litre cars, the intermediate speed-hold switch on automatic transmission models and for other auxiliary equipment such as a heated rear window switch, extra lighting controls, etc. There was no longer a cubby-hole on the driver's side of the dashboard. The remaining instruments and switches were neatly sited on a matt black painted (later covered in black figured Rexine) central panel with the ammeter, oil pressure, water temperature and fuel gauges situated neatly in a horizontal line only interrupted in the centre by a conventional Jaguar style lighting switch. Underneath the instruments there were a set of toggle switches covering the functions of interior lights, map reading light (bulb situated underneath the dashboard top rail), heater fan (two speed), wipers (two speeds), electric screen washers and panel lights (two intensities). These switches were positioned in two banks of three, the centre section occupied by the ignition

top left and right
Bench-seat Mark I automatic compared with manual version Mark II. Note the Mark II early-type Reutter recliners and special Henleys centre console, an optional extra only available in the early sixties.

above left and right
Dashboard layouts of the two models. The Mark I is an automatic version, the Mark II a very early model with recessed sun-visors and the original option of Derrington wood-rim steering wheel.

key switch, cigar lighter and the good old Jaguar push-button starter. Underneath the central black panel a plastic strip with white legend illuminated at night identified the functions of all the switches and controls. The whole centre panel could be hinged down to gain access to the rear of the instruments. A map shelf covered in black flock material was sited underneath the instrument panel, inside which could be found the pull lever to open the scuttle ventilator. On the passenger side of the dashboard a large glove box with downward-opening hinged lockable lid was fitted for passenger use. The inside, flock finished, had a large blue light illuminated at night with a simple push-button cut-off switch actuated by the lid. The lid itself had the unfortunate feature of having to be locked with the key to remain shut, there being no click catch or indeed handle to open the lid. This feature was particularly frustrating for a passenger requiring the glove-box open whilst the car was in motion, the key usually being attached to the same fob as the ignition key!

A new 17″ steering wheel was fitted with only two horizontal spokes and a neat chrome half horn ring – quite a break from Jaguar's traditional 'four spoker', as common a Jaguar feature as the push-button starter! The new wheel remained adjustable for reach as before. On the column there was a shrouded window display used for various functions depending on the specification of the car; on an automatic transmission model it showed the gear selection indicator, on overdrive cars it would simply state the word "overdrive" (illuminated whenever overdrive was engaged) and on non-overdrive cars the word "Jaguar" would be illuminated. In all cases the light would automatically dim whenever the car's external lights were switched on. On either side of the window there were two green arrows which illuminated and flashed when the indicators were in operation. The steering column was flanked by two stalks, the right hand one for the indicators and the left hand one for overdrive or automatic transmission selector. Very soon after production commenced, this particular positioning was altered, reversing the stalks – i.e. indicators to the left – apparently done for the benefit of export markets. The indicator stalk also doubled as a headlight flasher by pulling the stalk towards the driver.

Mark IIs were offered with a choice of three engine sizes to suit all markets and prospective owners. As well as the 2.4 and 3.4 litre versions as used in the earlier Mark I cars, a new high performance 3.8 litre model was available.

The 2.4 litre engine was substantially unaltered from the previous model but could now develop 120bhp instead of 112 at the same maximum revolutions (5,750rpm) by the fitting of the "B" type cylinder head giving improved breathing and torque. The pistons and connecting rods were of a different design to those used in the earlier engine, the pistons being of the semi-split-skirt type with four piston rings. The connecting rods had an oil squirt hole ($\frac{1}{32}$" diameter) drilled transversely into the oilway between the big and small ends. The original twin Solex downdraught carburettors with manual choke were retained. Because of increased weight in the new body shell amounting to just over 1cwt the 2.4 Mark II was not as quick as the older car and could not quite reach the magical 100mph, nor could the newer car claim the same economy as its predecessor or for that matter the larger engined Mark IIs. Because of this the 2.4 was never exported to America and was not readily available to motoring correspondents for road test purposes. The 2.4s were, however, still excellent value for money and provided executive travel at a very reasonable price. With a 0-50mph time of 12.7 seconds the 2.4 could not have been considered slow in relation to other cars. The model was well liked by owners, with over 25,170 being produced from 1959 to 1967. Very few 2.4s were produced with an automatic gearbox because of the amount of power soaked up by the transmission and most tended to be bought without some of the normal Jaguar optional extras like wire wheels.

The mid-range Mark II utilised the existing 3,442cc XK engine with the "B" type cylinder head and twin S.U. carburettors. A net output of 210bhp was available from this engine but the car again proved slightly slower than its predecessor because of increased body weight. The weight distribution between front and rear wheels was slightly altered and although top speed virtually remained unchanged, acceleration suffered compared with the Mark I, the Mark II being ½ second slower to 60mph and just under 3½ seconds slower to 100mph. The 3.4 litre was often referred to as the "sweetest" of the range as the car not only embodied superb performance, enough to match and better most of the opposition, but was also docile and made an ideal town carriage, particularly smooth and quiet. *Motor* referred to the 3.4 as "a car of brilliant versatility" and it was thought by many to have the ideal engine configuration for the XK unit, not subject to the vices of the other engines; a view I personally hold after owning most versions of the Mark II range. The only other mechanical change to the 3.4 involved the fitting of a shortened exhaust system with twin pipes directed to the rear nearside of the car and

Performance graph of the 2.4 Mark II engine.

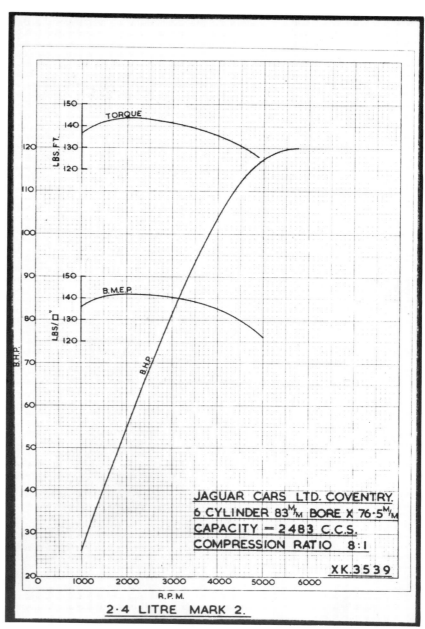

2·4 LITRE MARK 2.

with chromium trims. The difference in power between the 3.4 and 3.8 litre engines was not that noticeable at cruising speeds and as the 3.4 was cheaper to buy, slightly cheaper to insure and marginally more economical to maintain, it is no surprise that this was the most popular of the range, with over 28,600 produced from 1959 to 1967.

The 3.8 litre was the ultimate compact Jaguar saloon and is still the most desirable to own today. The 3,781cc engine was taken directly from the Mark IX and developed no less than 220bhp. The 3.8 litre was created by increasing the bore from 83 to 87mm (as previously done on some of the Jaguar racing engines); this was carried out by redesigning the block and using dry liners. The "B" type cylinder head was again employed with twin S.U. carburettors. All other aspects of the mechanics – the gearbox ratios, etc. – were retained from the 3.4 litre car although first gear was altered from 11.31 to 12.73. The Mark II, incidentally, was never offered with the triple carburettor XK 150 "S" engine. The 3.8 was a true 120mph performer with acceleration to match – 0-

60mph in only 8.5 seconds and a standing quarter mile in 16.3 seconds, with reasonable economy as well – *Sports Car Graphics* actually recorded 26mpg in a manual/overdrive 3.8 in 1962! No other production saloon car in the world could match the performance of a 3.8 litre Jaguar. It was certainly the fastest ever Jaguar saloon, a position it held until the introduction of the XJ12 in 1972. Nor could the competition rival the excellent value for money, the basic price of the 3.8 being only £1,780 (including purchase tax). Even in the North American market the 3.8 was cheap, costing only as much as the very cheapest Cadillac and yet being an undeniable status symbol. To quote the American *Road and Track*: "The car has an amazing effect on people. At the opera, theatre, parking lots, etc., the car is treated with deference reserved for very few makes of car. Car jaded kids turn their heads, filling station attendants almost beg to be allowed to lift the hood and dignified old ladies sneak looks at the nameplates and discreetly glance into the interior – the very essence of snob appeal." *Road and Track* went on to say, "it is a most exhilarating car to drive – to hold it on opposite lock through a corner is a dramatic experience." It was also considered by many to be a better car than the E Type! The phenomenal acceleration could better most sports cars of the day including the big Austin Healeys, the AC Ace Bristol and even the then new Aston Martin DB4. Occasionally 3.8s were modified by outside specialists by the fitting of a straight port head, triple HD8 S.U. carburettors, etc., which gave a boost to 250bhp, yielding a genuine 140mph and putting the car in line with the very best.

3.8s were not without their problems, high oil consumption and oil leakage being the most common. They were bought to be used and used they were, and many cars were not particularly good secondhand buys. Because of the tremendous torque on offer they were also more prone to broken exhaust mountings and similar disorders.

Moving on now to the rear suspension of the Mark II, this remained basically unaltered from the Mark I, the major change being the widening of the rear track by 3¼″ to 4ft 5½″, which still left the front track slightly wider. The rear track would have been widened further had it not been for the limiting factor of the body styling. The extra track altered the character and handling of the car dramatically, giving a more stable ride with increased resistance to roll when cornering. A Thornton Power-Lok limited slip differential (of American design) was a standard fitment to all 3.8 litre cars and was an optional extra on 3.4 litre cars, but it was never available for the 2.4 litre model. Completing the drive train, transmission options were as before, with the normal Moss four-speed gearbox with or without overdrive on fourth gear, although a high-ratio box and a three-speed Borg Warner automatic transmission were also available.

At the front the suspension was again similar to the Mark I but the roll tendency was reduced by slight changes in the geometry of the wishbones which gave the effect of raising the roll centre from ¾″ below ground level to 3¼″ above. Both wishbones were angled downwards and increased spacing between the ball joints was allowed. This was done by raising the inner pivot of the top wishbone and then lowering the ball joint on the bottom wishbone. Increasing the length of the upper wishbone reduced the steering swivel inclination from 7.3 to 4.5 degrees. Disc brakes on all models were retained with 11″ at the front and 11.375″ at the rear.

To complete the picture of the Mark II range the cars were initially available in a series of ten exterior colour schemes, three shades of grey (Pearl, the most popular on early cars, Warwick and Dove). Two shades of red (Carmen, the traditional sporting Jaguar colour of the fifties and sixties, and Imperial Maroon). The other colours available were Old English White, British Racing Green, Sherwood Green, Cotswold Blue and Indigo Blue. Other colours available to special order included Embassy Black and pure white although Jaguar continued their previous policy of supplying any colour to customer specification if required. Interior trim colours initially were grey, blue, red, green, champagne or tan, depending on exterior paint colour.

Prices for the "new" Mark II range in October 1959 were:-

2.4 Manual	**£1082** basic plus	**£451.19s.2d**	P.Tax =	**£1533.19s.2d**
2.4 Overdrive	**£1127** basic plus	**£470.14s.2d**	P.Tax =	**£1597.14s.2d**
2.4 Auto	**£1187** basic plus	**£495.14s.2d**	P.Tax =	**£1682.14s.2d**
3.4 Manual	**£1177** basic plus	**£491.10s.10d**	P.Tax =	**£1668.10s.10d**
3.4 Overdrive	**£1222** basic plus	**£510.5s.10d**	P.Tax =	**£1732.5s.10d**
3.4 Auto	**£1282** basic plus	**£575.5s.10d**	P.Tax =	**£1857.5s.10d**
3.8 Manual	**£1255** basic plus	**£524.0s.10d**	P.Tax =	**£1779.0s.10d**
3.8 Overdrive	**£1300** basic plus	**£542.15s.10d**	P.Tax =	**£1842.15s.10d**
3.8 Auto	**£1360** basic plus	**£567.15s.10d**	P.Tax =	**£1927.15s.10d**

Ace Wheeltrim option available on Jaguars compared with standard hubcaps and optional chrome Rimbellishers.

The most popular model sold in the first year of production was undoubtedly the 3.4 litre version, both the 2.4 and 3.4 litre models being readily available from January 1960. The 3.8 litre cars were not so easily available at this time, especially for the home market. Although actual figures are not known, hardly any 3.8s were produced without overdrive.

An extensive array of optional extras was available for the Mark II including the two styles of wheel trims, wire wheels, lockable filler cap, laminated windscreen, Witter tow-bar, various types of fitted radio (with the facility of an extension speaker on the rear parcel shelf), childproof locks on the rear doors, etc. A heated rear window was on offer, initially switched on automatically when the ignition was turned on, although a later variety was fitted with a dash-mounted on/off switch and warning light. More unusual options included an auxiliary fuel tank which occupied the space under the boot floor normally reserved for the spare wheel. The spare then had to be sited (with a special mounting bracket) on top of the boot floor, rendering the boot space virtually useless for luggage storage. From information available it would appear that this option was only ever ordered by a small number of foreign owners who needed to travel exceptionally long distances, and for competition cars. Another unusual and very rare option was the fitting of a steel sliding sunroof similar to that fitted on the Mark IX saloon. Jaguar even supplied a steering-wheel option, the normal black type being the standard equipment with a white plastic covered variety for export markets. Jaguar also instigated the manufacture of a special lightweight wood-rim wheel available to special order on all Mark IIs. This steering wheel, made by V.W. Derrington, weighed only 20oz (without the centre boss). The frame was made of polished Birmabright light alloy with rim of contrasting laminations of white obeechi and rich red mahogany, french polished to bring out the full beauty of the grain. Derrington claimed that their wood-rim wheels never got 'tacky'. Finger serrations on the underside of the rim helped the hands grip the shiny wood finish. This special steering wheel cost £12.15s.0d and took the standard Jaguar Mark II horn ring with plastic centre section. The centre fixing boss was metal with a black crackle finish and when fitted the column retained fore and aft adjustment as before. Other optional extras included front passenger safety belts, Sundym (tinted) windscreens and backlights and a special integrated ignition switch and steering wheel lock for certain export markets. One other extra was the availability of reclining front seats. Complete replacement seats were available of Reutter manufacture (part numbers BD 33065 lhs and BD 33064 rhs) and were basically of the same shape as the standard seats, even retaining the picnic tables, but had an elaborate heavy chromium bracket covering up the reclining mechanism to the seat sides. Kits were also available from Jaguar to convert existing seats to recliners.

A proud owner taking delivery of his Mark II outside the Browns Lane offices.

Development of the Legend

Although the concept of the Mark II design remained primarily the same throughout the eleven-year production run, there were numerous changes, some small, others highly significant, and it is thanks to the Jaguar factory records that it is possible to describe so many alterations to the range. As in the chapter on the development of the Mark I, chassis numbers are quoted wherever possible which may aid identification of particular cars.

Approximately two hundred cars were released during 1959. From January 1960 detailed modifications commenced, the very first of which concerned the silencer tailpipes, in future to be clipped to the silencers instead of welded. The new silencers had saw cuts at the ends of the exit pipes which were of increased length to take the tailpipes. After such a limited production period, owners had already started to complain about the inefficiency of the heating system. At the time Jaguar though the matter could be overcome by ensuring that the heater flap was closing fully. If the flap was found not to be closing correctly, the factory suggested to dealers that they make an extension strip from 16swg steel, welding it to the heater control lever bracket. At the same time Jaguar informed dealers that certain cars had left the factory without water drain holes in the rear tail lights, suggesting to them that they drill the necessary holes in the lenses to release excess water.

Also in January 1960 Jaguar issued a warning to dealers referring to complaints from customers that the oil pressure gauge was reading low, and suggesting the system be checked whenever cars were returned for service. By March complaints were still coming in and Jaguar decided to fit a revised gauge. The original gauge was calibrated to 100psi and at normal running pressures of around 40psi indicated only a quarter of the way up the scale. Many owners had become worried at this apparently low reading, complaining to Jaguar, although the reading was perfectly normal. Jaguar therefore re-calibrated the gauge to read a maximum pressure of 60psi so that normal running pressure would be indicated just over halfway up the scale. The new style gauge (part no. C.15473) necessitated a change in sensor for the

Late Mark II centre dash. Early cars had a 100psi oil pressure gauge and matt-black painted dashboard.

instrument and a kit (part no. C.15474) was available for dealers to change the gauge on existing cars, making the original 100psi gauge a rarity today. The modification commenced at chassis numbers 101446 (2.4 rhd), 125370 (2.4 lhd), 151003 (3.4 rhd), 175499 (3.4 lhd), 200668 (3.8 rhd), and 211867 (3.8 lhd). In the same month all cars received notched fan belts (part no. C.14535/1)from engine numbers KG.1891 (3.4) and LA.2330 (3.8).

In April a telescopic rear view mirror was fitted, and more significantly in May the steering column control stalks were reversed, the direction indicator and headlamp flasher to the left-hand side and the overdrive (or automatic transmission select) to the right, this apparently done to fall in line with the requirements of the export market. At the same time the engine breather was altered, venting into the carburettors, and the oil bath air cleaner originally fitted to the 3.4 and 3.8 litre engines was replaced by a large pancake paper-element cleaner sitting over the head. The oil bath air cleaner remained on 2.4 litre models until the Solex caburettors were abandoned much later in production. From chassis numbers 100731 (2.4 rhd). 125269 (2.4 lhd), 150562 (3.4 rhd), 175282 (3.4 lhd), 200301 (3.8 rhd) and 211041 (3.8 lhd) new front suspension springs were fitted, increased in length by ⅛″ .

July of 1960 saw the heater system modified by the fitting of a water valve to the unit. The valve, coupled to the temperature control flap, was operated by the hot-cold control in the driving compartment, the modification preventing warm air from entering the interior when not required. As the heater on the Mark II was never one of its better points, it is difficult to understand why warm air would have been a problem! However, in hot climates the situation may well have been more critical. In fact in the North American market some companies fitted crude home-grown air conditioning units involving the loss of most of the boot space, extensive modifications inside the car and a certain loss of bhp from the engine. July also saw a slight change to the dashboard – the matt black painted centre instrument panel gained a textured black Rexine covering. It had been found that the painted finish was scratched easily by dangling key fobs. Also at this time Jaguar incorporated in production a modification consisting of a breather pipe in the filler tank (adjacent to the vent pipe) and a non-vented fuel filler cap. This modification was brought about after complaints of petrol fumes.

In September at chassis numbers 103669 (2.4 rhd), 125711 (2.4 lhd), 152281 (3.4 rhd), 176023 (3.4 lhd), 201798 (3.8 rhd) and 213964 (3.8 lhd) the 4½J disc type wheels were replaced by wider 5J wheels (part no. C.16827). The type of wheel was stamped in the well of the rim and a further means of idenification is that the 5J wheels have an annular depression around the rim. At this time power steering also became available as an option on the Mark II. Through experience gained with the larger Mark IX saloon the system used was revised and adapted especially for the smaller Jaguar, hydraulic pressure was increased to 800/850psi from 650 and a smaller Burman recirculating steering box was used. Stiffer steering arms were employed at the same time. The system, available on the 3.4 and 3.8 litre models only, cost initially £77.18s.4d (including purchase tax). It was not available on the 2.4 because of the exhaust layout. Everyone who tried the Mark II with power steering liked it as it left the steering with plenty of feel, at the same time relieving the heaviness, particularly at low speeds, which was a constant characteristic of the Mark IIs and earlier Mark Is. One other alteration in September amounted to the fitment of the 4HA rear axle (in place of the 3HA) to 2.4 litre cars. In conjunction with this change, a shorter propshaft was fitted, standardising with the 3.4 and 3.8 litre cars – axle ratios remained unchanged.

In November the steering column was lowered slightly and the pendant type accelerator pedal was replaced by an organ type, which was more suitable for heel-and-toeing. The large rectangular ashtray on the transmission tunnel received attention after complaints from owners about stray ash spreading over the interior. The lid was therefore made spring loaded to the closed position. The recessed sun visors also received criticism from owners, the rather solid non-adjustable visors proving ineffective in

Early centre console ashtray.

Late model dashboard. Note shaping of steering wheel, reversion to simple type sun-visors and all-synchro style gearlever.

preventing glare and the driver's visor in particular getting in the way of the rear view mirror. From this time Jaguar fitted a more conventional visor hinged only at one side; the smaller and neater shape did not obstruct the use of the rear view mirror and the front seat passenger could adjust his/her visor easily to use the vanity mirror on the reverse side. After worries concerning wind noise and the flexing of front door window frames, Jaguar strengthened the frames, necessitating slight alterations to the front door wood cappings. On the mechanical side, alterations were also made in November, amounting to the fitting of a new S.U. fuel pump, the revised siting of the oil filter (facing downwards for better access) and the replacement of the metal brake fluid container with a plastic type. The above changes took place at engine numbers KG.4104 (3.4) and LA.7214 (3.8). At the same time the boss in the cylinder block provided for the fitting of a Bray electric engine heater was transferred from the left-hand side to the right, avoiding the obstruction from the exhaust pipes.

1961 saw numerous other modifications, starting in January with another attempt to stop engine oil leaks on the 3.8 litre engine by the fitting of a modified crankshaft rear cover. This was done in order to stop oil seeping when cars were parked on an incline facing uphill with the engine switched off. In February more rigid forged wishbones replaced the previous steel type and a kit was now available from the Factory to convert cars to power steering for £90. Also in that month a dipstick guide tube was fitted to the engine block to ensure easy replacement of the dipstick when checking the oil level. This was another modification carried out after numerous complaints from owners of the necessity of 'feeling' the dipstick back into position. This modification commenced at engine nos. KG.5366 (3.4) and LA.8593 (3.8). A stronger anti-roll bar was fitted to the front, improving the handling, and became a standard fitment, having previously been a special option.

During February metallic colour schemes became available for the exterior finish on Mark IIs. The initial colour range included Dark Green, Blue, Gunmetal, Silver Grey, Silver Blue and Bronze, all called Opalescent by Jaguar. This new range of colours proved popular with owners although prone to fading and difficult to match. The colour range was enlarged in October 1962 to include Golden Sand.

In June 1961 at engine numbers BG.8498 (2.4), KG.6738 (3.4) and LB.1850 (3.8) all engines were fitted with a modified sump introduced for the purpose of accomodating a larger capacity oil pump. The new sump was part no. C.17645 and the pump no. C.17655. In June rubber buffers were fitted to the outer rear corners of the front and rear door sills to eliminate movement of the doors when shut. Similar buffers were also added to the front wings to allow the bonnet edges to butt up against them when closed – these modifications took place from chassis numbers 105620 (2.4 rhd), 126080 (2.4 lhd), 153583 (3.4 rhd), 176602 (3.4 lhd),202910 (3.8 rhd) and 215650 (3.8 lhd). At the same chassis numbers the toughened glass windscreens were modified on all cars to include a special built-in 'zone' to ensure vision in the event of the windscreen being shattered.

In June 1961 all models received a modified fuel pump with a shorter cell housing. At the same time all cars received cast iron brake cylinder blocks, replacing the malleable iron. With this change the self-adjustment arrangement was modified, the spring washer no longer being used, and the

Early (left) and late model window-frames. Note the strengthening piece on the later model.

retraction being by a coil spring located in the piston. Also, whereas the original type had a separate piston and backing plate, the new type was of integral construction with no end plate. From chassis numbers 155965 (3.4 rhd), 177304 (3.4 lhd), 205364 (3.8 rhd) and 217573 (3.8 lhd) automatic transmission cars had an extended oil level dipstick fitted to the transmission, brought about by complaints of excessive heat entering the driving compartment. The new dipstick was of the remote type. Slightly earlier in production a modified radiator filler cap was fitted of a shallower type than previously, the filler neck also being suitably modified. A common cause of loss of pressure in the cooling system and subsequent water loss since on Mark IIs has been the incorrect fitting of the later shallow type filler cap to the deep type filler necked radiator.

In August, from engine numbers KG.9484 (3.4) and LA.5312 (3.8), modified inlet camshafts were fitted, having a hole drilled in the base of each cam to keep the noise level down, especially when cold. This modification was subsequently made to the 2.4 litre engines from number BH.2900 in October of that year. Returning to August, from chassis numbers 108998 (2.4 rhd), 126479 (2.4 lhd), 156343 (3.4 rhd), 177360 (3.4 lhd), 205633 (3.8 rhd) and 217696 (3.8 lhd), a self-adjusting handbrake mechanism was fitted. The adjustment occurred automatically as the linings wore and was effected by a spring loaded pawl rotating a toothed nut on the adjusting bolt when the handbrake off clearance between the disc and linings was in excess of a total of .006″. Here again a kit was available from the factory to convert earlier cars. Water deflectors were fitted to the front hubs at the same time. Certain complaints had reached Jaguar about wind noise from the front edges of the front doors, and it was recommended that a rubber sealing strip (part nos. BD.21361 left-hand side and BD.21362 right-hand side) be fitted to the forward edge of the doors adjacent to the top hinge.

In October of 1961 engines were modified to allow tension to be applied automatically to the fanbelt by means of a spring-loaded jockey pulley (part number C.18733). Also a modified rear end cover with provision for an asbestos oil seal was fitted to all crankshafts from engine numbers BH.4551 (2.4), LH.2794 (3.4) and LB.8247 (3.8), part number C.19648. The earlier scroll type seal had proved another cause of oil seepage from the XK engine unit. Larger and stronger propshaft universal joints were supplied on all cars at the

Special Jaguar seat-belts available on all Jaguars of the period.

same time and from engine numbers BH.4553 (2.4), KH.2794 (3.4) and LB.8359 (3.8) a modified camshaft cover was fitted over the exhaust camshaft to improve oil sealing.

Referring now to January 1962, front seat belt attachment points were provided from chassis numbers 111418 (2.4 rhd), 126652 (2.4 lhd), 158371 (3.4 rhd), 177753 (3.4 lhd), 207313 (3.8 rhd) and 219801 (3.8 lhd). At the same time Jaguar announced the supply of their own brand seat belts with 'Jaguar' motifs, part nos. 9212 front seat (lap and diagonal) and 9213 rear seat (diagonal only). Prior to this time an owner requesting the fitment of belts had to put up with crude brackets drilled through the floor in the middle of the rear passenger footwells.

In February a high output dynamo became an option on 3.4 and 3.8 litre cars, and a new sealing ring of steel and asbestos material was fitted between the exhaust manifolds and downpipes on all models. In March a modified section fanbelt (part no. C.19523) was fitted to 2.4 litre engines from engine number BH.5365. The dynamo, crankshaft and water pump pulleys were differently machined to suit the new belt. This modification was extended to 3.4 and 3.8 litre engines at engine numbers KH.4023 and LC.1672 respectively in April of that year. At the end of March a modified sump was fitted to all engines, part number C.19922, from engine numbers BH.5853 (2.4), KH.4020 (3.4) and LC.1506 (3.8). Finally in April a modified brake servo unit (part number C.19612) was fitted to all cars, incorporating a two-stage air valve to reduce noise upon brake application.

In September 1962 Jaguar fitted Brico Maxiflex scraper rings in a further attempt to reduce oil consumption on the 3.8 litre cars. This reputedly reduced the average oil consumption figure to around 400mpp. Further in September all right hand drive cars received sealed beam headlights (part no. 8386) from chassis numbers 112995 (2.4), 160201 (3.4) and 208535 (3.8). In November at engine numbers BH.7969 (2.4), KH.7063 (3.4) and LC.4265 (3.8), the oil filter mounting was modified, retained by five bolts instead of the previous four, and a rubber seal was fitted to the oil pressure relief valve and also to the balance valve. Announced on the same date from engine numbers BH.7671, KH.7310 and LC.4461, oil level dipsticks received lengthened handles to clear the exhaust. Finally, in 1964, at chassis numbers 114063 (2.4 rhd), 126900 (2.4 lhd), 161400 (3.4 rhd), 178733 (3.4 lhd), 209382 (3.8 rhd) and 221881 (3.8 lhd) a modified upper steering column was fitted enabling the Waso combined ignition switch and steering lock to be fitted as an optional extra. This new extra replaced the normal ignition switch on the dashboard and was mounted on an extension arm attached to the steering column below the steering wheel – the traditional Jaguar styled push button starter on the dashboard remained operative.

In January 1963 a reinforcement bracket was fitted to the Panhard rod mounting from chassis number 114110 (2.4), 161442 (3.4) and 209424 (3.8), part no. BD.24283. The Panhard rod mounting proved a constant source of trouble from the introduction of the original Mark I, throughout the production run of the Mark II and into the 240/340 range. Lubrication of the front suspension was improved at this time by putting nylon washers in the top and bottom wheel swivels and tie rod seals. The idea was that excess grease could easily escape without damaging the seals but this was not totally successful as dirt could stop grease reaching the ball joints. The steering idler assembly was given taper roller bearings also during this month. In February more durable Girling shock absorbers were supplied to improve the ride generally, particularly improving the control on very rough roads as the new dampers' fullest travel was hardly ever used. During this month, on cars for export to Italy, the headlights had to have revised wiring to 'flash' when the lights were off or in main beam positions only.

In March, commencing at engine numbers BH.8488 on 2.4 litre cars and KH.7999 on 3.4 litre cars, all engines received the modified Maxiflex compression ring previously used in 3.8 litre cars only. At chassis numbers

114849 (2.4 rhd), 127055 (2.4 lhd), 162488 (3.4 rhd), 178974 (3.4 lhd), 230140 (3.8 rhd) and 222241 (3.8 lhd) cars were fitted with upper and lower steering columns of the same type as used on the Mark X saloon. At the same time rear seat legroom was improved by the fitting of new style front seats with cutaways in the seat backs for the rear passengers' feet. The new seats could still be specified with or without reclining mechanisms and were utilised from chassis numbers 115017 (2.4 rhd), 127082 (2.4 lhd), 162688 (3.4 rhd), 179029 (3.4 lhd), 230325 (3.8 rhd) and 222338 (3.8 lhd).

In April 1963 modified door light frames incorporating flocked rubber channel inserts and new window glass were introduced at chassis numbers 114992 (2.4 rhd), 127075 (2.4 lhd), 162651 (3.4 rhd), 179010 (3.4 lhd), 230298 (3.8 rhd) and 222289 (3.8 lhd). This modification helped to reduce wind noise and water penetration to the inside of the door frame. Also in April all models received a new type of dynamo, C.40L (2.4 litre cars) and C.42 on 3.4 and 3.8 litre models – this alteration necessitated a change in control box. The new dynamo was of a higher output, first available in February 1962 as an option but now standardised. At this time a new distributor was fitted, waterproofed in August by the fitting of a rubber cap over each plug lead and the H.T. lead where they entered the cap.

In May at chassis numbers 115183 (2.4 rhd), 127126 (2.4 lhd), 162955 (3.4 rhd), 179116 (3.4 lhd), 230496 (3.8 rhd) and 222524 (3.8 lhd) a new radiator pressure cap of 9lbs pressure was fitted with a new top hose and hose clip. In the same month all right hand drive cars were fitted with a rubber dust excluder behind the headlamp outer rim, effective from chassis numbers 115237, 163015 and 230538. An improved water pump was fitted to 3.4 and 3.8 litre engines which had a falling flow effect when the engine was working hard above 5,000rpm. A large diameter propshaft was fitted at this time (3″) with sealed-for-life universal joints, and finally, in September, 3.4 and 3.8 litre cars received spark plug leads of increased length with a revised 'run' taking effect from engine numbers KJ.1121 and LC.6993.

In October Jaguar made another change to the radiator pressure cap decreasing the pressure to 7lbs. At this time a new style steering wheel was fitted to all models exactly as fitted to the Mark X and all other subsequent saloons up to the introduction of the XJ6 series 1. Although retaining the half horn ring, the new wheel had a 'live' centre horn button and revised centre span spoke shaping. This standardisation of steering wheels took place from chassis numbers 116114 (2.4 rhd), 127312 (2.4 lhd), 164002 (3.4 rhd), 179499 (3.4 lhd), 231586 (3.8 rhd) and 353182 (3.8 lhd) although a few cars prior to these numbers were modified without the 'live' centre button. The white (export) wheel was now dropped but the Derrington woodrim wheel could still be supplied. Lastly, in October, a new front suspension cross-member mounting (part no. C.23314) was fitted with improved bonding, identifiable by a small cross moulded in the rubber.

In November the electric clock fitted to the rev. counter incorporated a rectifier to reduce fouling of the contact points within the clock. This modification took effect around the same time as the oil level dipstick was altered, from engine numbers BH.7671 (2.4), KH.7310 (3.4) and LC.4461 (3.8).

Modifications continued into 1964, when in January grease nipples were fitted to the front wheel bearings on steel wheeled cars, eliminating the need to dismantle the hub. In March all Mark IIs were fitted with improved interior lamps in the centre pillars, which required a re-designed mounting and capping, effective from chassis numbers 116999 (2.4 rhd), 127430 (2.4 lhd), 165424 (3.4 rhd), 179656 (3.4 lhd), 231931 (3.8 rhd) and 223349 (3.8 lhd). In the same month, in a further attempt to curb excessive oil consumption on 3.8 litre engines, the pistons were modified to allow excess oil passage back into the sump by way of a chamfer and drain hole below the piston oil control rings. Thus oil that was picked up by the ring could return to the sump easily. By April all models were standardised with the 'S' Series by the fitting of revised oil cleaners (part no. C.20525), the same standardisation applying to flywheels (part no. C.23328) from engine numbers KJ.4037 (3.4) and LC.8990 (3.8).

In May 1964 the radiator pressure cap was again changed to a pressure of 4lb in line with S Types from chassis numbers 117502 (2.4 rhd), 127509 (2.4 lhd), 166390 (3.4 rhd), 179795 (3.4 lhd), 232536 (3.8 rhd) and 223530 (3.8 lhd). At this time a new S.U. fuel pump was fitted and an 8 amp fuse was introduced into the intermediate speed hold circuit (automatic transmission cars) and the control circuit on overdrive models – all modifications again in standardisation with the S Type saloons. A minor modification was also made to the interior carpets at this time – from chassis numbers 117556 (2.4 rhd), 127520 (2.4 lhd), 166511 (3.4 rhd), 179831 (3.4 lhd), 232601 (3.8 rhd) and 223585 (3.8 lhd) a one-piece front floor and toe board carpet was featured. Stud fasteners replaced the 'bow' type formerly employed. Following cases of severe salt corresion affecting the attachment brackets for the vacuum reservoir, Jaguar recommended to dealers that a new fixing rod assembly became standard on all Mark IIs from chassis numbers 116200 (2.4 rhd), 127334 (2.4 lhd), 164495 (3.4 rhd), 179522 (3.4 lhd), 231603 (3.8 rhd) and 223125 (3.8 lhd). Around the same time, in June, all cars were fitted with revised brake bleed nipples, repositioned from the outside to the inside of each caliper, hydraulic pipes being also modified to suit.

In August of 1964 all engines were fitted with lifting brackets to facilitate engine removal, the incorporation of the brackets necessitating the use of lengthened cylinder head studs and a modified conduit for the spark plug leads. This addition took effect from engine numbers BJ.3662 (2.4), KJ.5520 (3.4) and LE.1218 (3.8). A modified front timing cover allowing the front oil seal to be changed without removing the cover was fitted to all engines at this time.

At this time, apparently due to short supply of materials, the following cars were supplied with front floor carpets bearing heel pads of PVC in place of hardura:

2.4 litre	117269 to 117555 rhd, 127465 to 127519 lhd
3.4 litre	165960 to 166510 rhd, 179702 to 179830 lhd
3.8 litre	232270 to 232600 rhd, 223428 to 223584 lhd

For October, further standardisation took place with the introduction of the S Type sump pan to all Mark IIs, part number C.24502 from engine numbers BJ.3575 (2.4), KJ.5520 (3.4) and LE.1214 (3.8). In the same month the chromium 'Automatic' emblem on the boot was discontinued from all automatic transmission cars, effective from chassis numbers 117901 (2.4 rhd), 127605 (2.4 lhd), 167287 (3.4 rhd), 179943 (3.4 lhd), 233039 (3.8 rhd) and 223837 (3.8 lhd). All subsequent boot panels manufactured had the appropriate drill holes omitted. At chassis numbers 118052 (2.4 rhd) and 127636 (lhd), 167631 (3.4 rhd) and 179994 (lhd), 233264 (3.8 rhd) and 223960 (lhd) shields were fitted to the inside of the brake discs to reduce the tendency for the inner brake pad to wear more quickly than the outer pad. After a further twenty or so cars had been produced a new upper universal joint was fitted to the lower steering column, the joint from then on being in two halves.

For December 1964 additional paint colours were added to the range: Warwick Grey, Indigo Blue and Pale Primrose. Another attempt was made to aid cooling by the fitting of a modified, larger radiator block (C.24916) and fan cowl (C.24965) to 3.4 and 3.8 litre models. This modification took place from chassis numbers 167989 (3.4 rhd), 180035 (3.4 lhd), 233460 (3.8 rhd) and 224023 (3.8 lhd). One week later the same modification was carried out to the 2.4 litre cars from chassis numbers 118268 (rhd) and 127679 (lhd).

In January 1965 the radio aperture finisher panel was the subject of modification with relocated fixing studs at 6¼″ centres instead of 5⁷⁄₁₆″. In April all models received a new type Lucas 5SJ screenwasher system with a

For many the ultimate Mark II look, the thick-bumpered variety with chrome wire wheels and white-wall tyres.

high density polythene reservoir instead of the previous glass type. The new system was not now automatic and therefore only remained operational as long as the dashboard switch was held in the raised position. The new unit was applicable from chassis numbers 118878 (2.4 rhd), 127760 (2.4 lhd), 168957 (3.4 rhd), 180137 (3.4 lhd), 233919 (3.8 rhd) and 224086 (3.8 lhd). At the same time the water drain tube from the battery tray was lengthened to stop drainage on to one of the brake pipes.

Water penetrating the distributor still seemed to be a problem for in June Jaguar started to fit a waterproof cover, retained in position by the distributor cap, this modification taking place from engine numbers BJ.4484 (2.4), KJ.6898 (3.4) and LE.2047 (3.8). In the same month all cars were fitted with a revised gauze for the scuttle ventilator lid. At engine numbers BJ.4609, KJ.7071 and LE.2123 respectively, the oil filler cap received an 'O' ring (part no. C.25480) replacing the fibre type. Jaguar also at this time installed a modified automatic transmission unit (C.25615) to improve the shift quality.

In September cars for the U.S. market were equipped with a hazard warning system as standard equipment. An extra flasher unit was situated behind the instrument panel and an auxiliary toggle switch and warning lamp were fastened under the dashboard on the driver's side. The main change in September, however, involved the introduction of a new manual gearbox which had initially been used on other Jaguar models several months earlier. The adoption of this new box with synchromesh on all four forward gears made a very worthwhile improvement to all Jaguar cars. The previous Moss gearbox had stemmed from a 1940s design with synchromesh that could easily be beaten on the upper three ratios. For silent running the new box was assembled in a casing of cast iron. Very large synchromesh units, of 3.057in mean cone diameter were fitted to all intermediate gears. They were of the baulk ring inertia lock type, designed for rapid and easy gear changing at maximum engine revs. For accurate poitioning and positive engagement, the sliding dog members had detent notches incorporated internally, instead of on the selector shafts. The operating gear and the rubber mounted gear lever were carried on a pressure diecast top cover of aluminium. The solid layshaft was integral with its gears and ran on crowded needle roller bearings on a dead shaft. The new gearbox was a tremendous improvement on the old Moss 'box but still suffered to some extent from excessive travel from first to second gear, although easier and smoother changes were possible with little apparent whine, a familiar characteristic of the old unit. The new gearbox (part no. C.25867) was installed from chassis numbers 119200 (2.4 rhd), 127822 (2.4 lhd), 169341 (3.4 rhd), 180188 (3.4 lhd), 234125 (3.8 rhd) and 224150 (3.8 lhd). The all-synchromesh gearbox was as fitted to the Mark X and S Type saloons and a close-ratio version was available with similar ratios to those used in the E Type sports car. In conjunction with the gearbox change, a revised diaphragm clutch with self-adjusting slave cylinder, operating rod and adjuster including the clutch fork return spring and clutch housing were fitted. The new clutch was a lot lighter and compensated automatically for normal wear and tear in use, although this type was later abandoned in 1968.

In November, all Mark IIs had the rear quarter light screws coated with Loctite after many complaints that the catches worked loose and in some cases even dropped off! The front quarterlights were also modified to include an extra notched opening. At the same time Jaguar started to fit paper-element oil filters to all cars leaving the Factory.

In March 1966, Mark IIs from chassis numbers 119356 (2.4 rhd), 127868 (2.4 lhd), 169632 (3.4 rhd), 180262 (3.4 lhd), 234395 (3.8 rhd) and 224207 (3.8 lhd) were fitted with redesigned handbrake mechanism retraction plates giving improved alignment of the pad carriers. In April Black was added to the standard exterior colour range (previously an extra cost option) and at chassis

One of the last true Mark IIs, a 1967 example retaining the thick bumpers but with horn grilles instead of fog lights.

number 119581 (2.4 rhd), 127912 (2.4 lhd), 170091 (3.4 rhd), 180310 (3.4 lhd), 234715 (3.8 rhd) and 224271 (3.8 lhd), all cars were fitted with a revised direction indicator switch operated through a freely rotated castellated nylon striker ring in direct contact with the striker attached to the column, the result being less travel to engage the indicator switch and a more positive motion. Around the same chassis numbers Lucas 9H horns were fitted replacing the previous 618U type, and from chassis numbers 119902, 127998, 170565, 180398, 235046 and 224417 respectively the heated rear window had a control switch, warning light and relay with resistance included in the electrical circuit. The warning light was dimmed when the side lights were switched on and the switch and light were attached to the driver's side of the instrument panel.

September of 1966 saw significant changes made to the Mark II range in an attempt to keep them competitively priced. Jaguar decided that economy measures were the order of the day to maintain their market position. A new style Ambla (plastic) upholstery material was used as standard for all seats although leather could still be supplied as an extra cost option. The small picnic tables set into the rear of the front seats were deleted and the headlining and sunvisors were of a cheaper material, standardising with the S Type saloons. Externally, differences amounted to the loss of the twin inset foglamps at the front, reverting to the previous practice of fitting dummy horn grilles (as on export cars), although here again these could still be supplied as an accessory, revised door top chrome beading with outer rubber seals fitted replacing the previous weather strip. The centre 'B' post door pillar chrome trim was from then on moulded in one piece, whereas previously the small (just under 1½″) chrome beading had been a separate item to the main vertical trim section.

In December the 2.4 received a modified tail pipe arrangement, incorporating a separate chrome plated portion and the use of circular rubber mountings, identical with that already used on 3.4 and 3.8 litre cars, all taking effect from chassis numbers 120291 (rhd) and 128054 (lhd). Two weeks later the 3.4 and 3.8 litre cars were modified and tail-pipes were made detachable, secured by self-tapping screws, effective from chassis numbers 170881 (3.4 rhd) and 180474 (3.4 lhd), and 235152 (3.8 rhd) and 224156 (3.8 lhd).

In the same month 2.4 litre cars were fitted with a redesigned crankshaft vibration damper from engine number BJ.6132, incorporating an integral fanbelt pulley and replacing the original two-piece unit and hub. The brake fluid warning light also received attention and in future was to have a rubber sleeve (part no. C.2607) fitted over the terminals to avoid the possibility of a short circuit.

By March 1967 exterior painted colour schemes had been modified, and in some cases rationalised, to the following: Opalescent Silver Blue, Silver Grey, Maroon, Dark Green and Golden Sand. Non-metallic colours were Primrose, Indigo Blue, Sherwood Green (to special order only), Carmen Red, Willow Green, Warwick Grey, Black and Honey Beige. Further standardisation took place by the fitting of the S Type power steering box and pump to 3.4 and 3.8 litre cars at chassis numbers 171101 (3.4 rhd), 180529 (3.4 lhd) and 235196 (3.8 rhd) and 224588 (3.8 lhd). This new Marles Varamatic system gave more feel and lighter steering, reducing the number of turns lock to lock. The Marles steering was in fact fitted to very few Mark IIs before the introduction of the 240/340 models and is therefore a rare find today.

From engine numbers BJ.5736 (2.4), KJ.8772 (3.4) and LE.3443 (3.8), circlips were fitted to the valve guides to ensure positive location in the cylinder head. From July all Mark II road wheels (disc type) were changed in favour of the 420 style (part no. C.27022). Around this time the boot lock was at long last altered in an attempt to stop the lid flying open on rough road surfaces. Last of all, the final production run of Mark IIs incorporated Velcro nylon strip carpet fastenings instead of studs.

After a spectacular production run of eight years Mark II manufacture terminated in September 1967 in favour of the 240/340 model range.

Mark IIs on Trial

Let us now assess the Mark II saloon on the road and discuss the cars with their owners. As pointed out earlier, in this book I wanted to avoid reproducing contemporary road test reports but I think it would prove significant to mention a survey carried out by *Motor Sport* in June 1962 with the help of a cross-section of then new Jaguar compact saloon owners.

Of those owners contacted 72.4% were well satisfied with service from Jaguar dealers and/or factory. 19.8% were dissatisfied, only 2.8% did their own servicing and general maintenance and 5% made no comment. Such a high percentage of dealer satisfaction was a credit to Jaguar.

Owners were asked about extras fitted to their cars and by far the most popular item specified was Koni adjustable shock absorbers, at 11.9% of the survey. Next came the high ratio steering box, with 10.2% of owners preferring this option (over 7% of them on 3.4 and 3.8 litre cars). Cylinder head modifications accounted for 3.4%, modified exhaust systems 4.5%, and 2.8% of 2.4 litre car car owners had had different carburettors fitted. More conventional options like wire wheels, overdrive, etc., were not covered in any great depth by the survey. The above seems to identify the Mark II owner as a sporting motorist not afraid of having his car slightly modified.

Participants in the survey were also asked about faults and complaints on their Mark IIs. The commonest complaints concerned timing chain adjustment, incorrect carburettor settings, trouble with the automatic choke (on 3.4 and 3.8 litre cars only) remaining on too long, general oil leakage and poor oil consumption. Many minor complaints included electric clocks not working, speedometer cables 'dancing', headlamps of insufficient brightness, etc. 15.8% complained of poor synchromesh on the gearbox and a further 3.9% of a noisy gearbox. Generally speaking, 15% of owners complained about bodywork defects, especially water leaks and 10.7% specifically about rust, poor chromium plate and ill-fitting items. Despite the above comments 78% would buy the Mark II again. From the remaining owners in the survey 2.8% would have purchased a Rover next, 2.3% a Mercedes-Benz, 1.7% a Volvo, 1.7% a Ford, 3% a Lotus, 1.3% an Aston Martin, 1.3 % a VW/Sunbeam/ Alvis/Alfa Romeo or Fiat, and 2.8% were unsure. Overall, the survey showed that owners were well satisfied with their Mark IIs and perhaps being a little over-critical, for how many of the alternative makes mentioned were true competitors of the small Jaguar? To quote *Autocar* of 21st October 1960, "No-one in the world could find such excellent value as the Mark II models represent."

Without wishing to bore readers too much with other magazine comments, I would just like to mention some points from a more unusual roadtest in *Commercial Motor* of 28th August 1967, assessing the 3.8 Mark II as a 'fleet' company car. To quote, "Running a Jaguar is the ambition of many car drivers and one of the major status symbols." On their test fuel consumption came out (over 1,840 miles) to an average of 18.7mpg with a best figure of 23 on a 500 mile town and motorway journey and a worst of 15mpg on a 45 mile town journey. Their evaluation panel came out with the following rating on the 3.8 litre car:

	(Maximum points 100)
Handling and roadholding	**90 points**
Lightness and accuracy of hand controls	**75 points**

Response and lightness of foot controls	**90 points**
Mechanical quietness	**95 points**
Driver comfort	**90 points**
Heating and Ventilation	**55 points**
Visibility (including mirrors)	**65 points**
Standard of lighting	**100 points**
Convenience (response/safety of catches, switches, etc.)	**95 points**
Placing and legibility of instruments and switches.	**95 points**

Mostly high marks when one considers that at this time the Mark II concept was eight years old. Marks for heating ventilation and visibility are understandably low.

Moving on now to the Mark II today, I first contacted John Hardwick, who has owned a 2.4 litre version from new in August 1967. Mr Hardwick, now retired, had never before owned a Jaguar but was initially 'sold' on the idea when a neighbour purchased a 2.4 litre Mark II in 1964. Mr Hardwick bought his car just before the changeover to the 240. Registered RDT 579F, it was one of the last to leave Jaguar, chassis number 121709, and has the characteristic Ambla upholstery and other late Mark II features. Finished in Willow Green with black interior, the car is the standard overdrive model (without a radio) but with the addition of foglamps and Ace Turbo wheel trims.

John Hardwick chose a 2.4 litre as this seemed the best engine for his needs; not a fast driver, he preferred the sedate approach to motoring, and apart from regular annual trips to Scotland the car was normally only used locally. The 2.4 had covered a total of 70,000 miles and was regularly serviced by only one garage. John particularly liked the smoothness of the ride and quality of finish. Being proud of his Jaguar he enjoyed driving 'her' and although he had thought several times of exchanging 'her' for a more modern, smaller car, at the end of the day he remained faithful to the Mark II. In John's own words, "Where else could I find such quality and refinement at anything like a reasonable price today?"

RDT 579F has been completely reliable for Mr Hardwick although he has has often complained of poor fuel consumption, most probably due to the type of driving (short local runs). His only criticism concerns the bodywork, which has now started to show signs of the dreaded rot in most places. During its life, the 2.4 has had new sills and various other repair panels but never a total respray; the car still passes its M.O.T. but soon will be in need of major surgery at the back end and around the front wing areas.

John Hardwick's Willow Green 2.4 Mark II.

Mr Hardwick gave me the opportunity to drive his 2.4 Mark II and assess for myself the smaller engined late model saloon. My initial impressions were basically favourable although I did not take kindly to the smell of the Ambla upholstery (not quite the same as the aroma of leather). Nevertheless the seats were comfortable and felt a little higher than on other Mark IIs. Apart from the Ambla upholstery and the nylon carpeting, the interior is as on any other Mark II, although perhaps the woodwork does not quite have the depth of finish. On the road the car was quiet and relatively responsive although I have driven faster 2.4s. It was shod with cross-ply tyres which certainly seemed to help the ride, and the steering was definitely not as heavy because of this. The all-synchromesh gearbox was a joy to use and I rarely had to worry about gear-crash. At the time the overdrive did not appear to be working and thus at anything above 70mph the engine became noisy. A visible tell-tale of the smaller engine was the rev. counter, indicating 3,000rpm at only 55mph! At normal speeds and at tickover the engine was remarkably quiet and generally the car behaved well.

Apart from a slight tear in the driver's seat and normal wear to the driver's carpet, the interior had kept remarkably well, I doubt whether leather would have looked so well under similar circumstances! Externally, the car could now do with a respray, the original paint dulling and the resprayed areas being of a slightly different shade. The chromework is immaculate and the car sits well with none of the usual suspension droop. Altogether the car was nice to drive and Mr Hardwick intends to continue using the Mark II as everyday transport. With a little care and time, this particular 2.4 could be brought back to its previous stately condition.

Next I spoke to Harry Beaumont who knows a lot about Jaguars and currently owns a 1965 3.4 litre Mark II. Harry is an ex-mechanic from Appleyards Garage of Leeds (Jaguar distributors for many years and owned by that famous rally driver of the forties and fifties Ian Appleyard). Now retired, Harry cherishes his immaculate Mark II, registered EWW 402C, finished in opalescent Golden Sand with red interior. Harry purchased the car approximately three years ago from its one previous lady owner. It has covered a genuine 40,000 miles from new and is totally original except for a part respray necessary due to the usual rust problems around the sills, wheel-arches and spat areas.

The 3.4 Mark II automatic.

Harry has admired Mark IIs for many years, since he first started working on them back in the sixties. The car is not in everyday use, Harry wishing to keep it in as near original condition as possible. However, he does really enjoy driving it. He considers the Mark II to have few vices, one of the major ones being the heating system, poor even by sixties standards. Pretty common minor faults he has experienced with his car, and others he has maintained, include the usual Panhard rod mounting breakage and knocks and groans from the rear suspension. The engine of Harry's car was exceptionally quiet and ticked over at astonishingly low revs. Harry has never believed the commonly held assumption that one should hear the tappets on a Jaguar engine. He also considers the Mark II an ideal 'classic' car, being small, relatively economical and above all very easy to maintain despite the cramped engine compartment.

I next spoke to Malcolm Buckeridge, who has his own business specialising in the maintenance and restoration of Jaguars. Malcolm has owned a total of twelve Mark IIs plus two Mark Is and currently runs a 3.8 litre Mark II of 1963 vintage, registered 2 KOV, which he purchased back in 1977. The car is finished in gunmetal with beige interior and is equipped with automatic transmission, heated rear window, power assisted steering and the unusual addition of a hazard warning system fitted from new by the first owner.

The car was originally supplied by Mists of Birmingham and has done a reputedly genuine mileage of 65,000, of which 12,000 miles have been in Malcolms hands. Since purchasing the car Malcolm has used it extensively up to a couple of years ago when it was taken off the road for a rebuild. Although still running well at the time, the bodywork was starting to suffer and the metallic paintwork in particular had faded badly.

Whilst it was in use Malcolm Buckeridge found his 3.8 very reliable and a pleasurable car to drive. He particularly likes the 3.8 litre engine as it has that much more torque than the 3.4 litre cars, and he is also a strong believer in automatic gearboxes, the 3.8 supplying ample power to overcome any loss in horsepower through the transmission. 2 KOV returns around 200mpp of oil, average for a 3.8 litre engine, and about 14/15mpg of petrol in normal town driving, rising to just over 20mpg on a run. As the Mark II is traditionally a heavy car to steer, Malcolm has found the power assistance a boon, especially when parking, although he does think the system lacks feel, especially at speeds in excess of 70mph.

Malcolm claims that he has always found the Mark II a very economical car to maintain with most parts readily available new or secondhand at reasonable prices providing one looks around. Most aspects of the mechanicals are easy to work on although the engine bay is rather cramped and many owners would do best to bring in professional help for engine rebuilds, clutch removal, etc. Malcolm considers that the braking system is only just adequate for a car of such power and he would like to improve the steering. On the other side of the coin, Malcolm finds the heating system on his Mark II very good and because of the built-in heated rear window, 2 KOV does not suffer from misting (a common complaint with the model).

As an everyday classic Malcolm finds the Mark II ideal and he thinks of the car as a grand touring two-plus-two saloon rather than a four door family car. Rear seat legroom is a little cramped but is more than adequate for children up to the age of about twelve. He finds the boot space limited.

Malcolm Buckeridge is a staunch supporter of the Jaguar marque and in particular the Mark II saloon. He considers his 3.8 can still outperform most modern equivalents on top speed, acceleration and quality of workmanship. Apart from his other Jaguar, a Mark IX, he cannot think of any other car he would willingly change to. 2 KOV is now undergoing a rebuild to bring it back to its former glory. Now restored bodily, the car has been resprayed in Carmen Red and will soon be back on the road in regular use. In the meantime Malcolm is driving a 2.4 litre Mark II as he openly agrees that he can't leave a good thing alone!

The Final Phase

The final phase of the Mark II design came in September 1967 with the introduction of the 240 and 340 models, the Mark II name finally being dropped although the new models retained most of the original design concepts. Mark IIs, however, continued to be sold into 1968 as cars were still in dealers' hands. The latest car registered known to the author was a 2.4 in March 1968.

Jaguar had been pursuing a policy of what can only be termed as saloon car market saturation in the sixties, with no less than seven Jaguar models (three Mark IIs, two S Types, the 420 and the 420G), not to mention the two Daimler equivalents (the 2.5 V8 and Sovereign) – a total of nine model series giving an unbelievable choice of eighteen different standard production models. With the advent of the mid-range models, the S Types and 420s, the Mark II had slowly been downgraded, and many owners who had previously purchased 3.4 or 3.8 litre Mark IIs were now moving 'up' to the S Type equivalents with more passenger comfort, boot space and the sophisticated rear suspension which gave a far superior ride. The Mark II did, however, remain popular with the more sporting motorist, maintaining its position as the true Jaguar sports saloon in both looks and feel.

The Jaguar 240. Note the thinner bumpers and new style hub-caps common to other Jaguars of the period.

To keep the Mark IIs competitive in price, Jaguar had to take certain economy measures and rationalise the model range. To this end they discontinued production of the 3.8 litre Mark II, as this model more than the others clashed with the 3.8 litre S Type and the larger engined (4.2 litres) 420, which by this time was getting firmly established in the U.S.A. as the 'best Jaguar saloon yet'. The 2.4 and 3.4 litre cars continued in production, although with various changes to keep the selling price down. The changes (or modifications depending on your point of view) caused quite a stir at the time. Many felt that Jaguar had cheapened the image of the cars too much. Such items as the Ambla upholstery instead of traditional leather had not received much publicity when introduced on the last of the Mark IIs, but on the 240/340 models it caused an outcry, and at least one comment was passed that the small Jaguar saloon 'was no more than a sportier Ford Zephyr'. Such criticisms were perhaps unfair, as Jaguar still retained a quality of finish superior to that of most British mass-produced cars.

Let us now look at the changes that took place on the introduction of the new models, starting with the exterior bodywork. It is often said that the thickness of the body panels was slightly reduced. There is no evidence to prove this but it is possible that the presses had worn and were causing excessive pressure to be applied. The traditional thick bumper bars were replaced by a slimline type, similar to those used on the S Type and 420 models, with matching over-riders. Because of the thinner bumpers, the front and rear body valances were modified accordingly. The hubcaps were also changed to ones of the same design as were fitted on all Jaguar saloons at the time, with a black plastic centre depicting a gold Jaguar head. Rimbellishers were an option rarely seen on 240 or 340 models. Horn grilles continued to be used at the front with the option of flush-fitting fog lamps at extra cost.

As for the interior, Ambla upholstery was standard, as previously mentioned, with the extra cost option of leather (rarely specified on 240s, but occasionally on 340s). The veneering of the woodwork altered, with less 'figuring', and the veneer was of a much lighter shade. Tufted nylon carpets replaced the more traditional weave previously used. Inside the boot, the now famous Jaguar boxed tool-kit was still fitted, but with a plastic moulded case instead of the Mark II's wood and metal case. The new plastic box was standardised for the S Types and 420s by July 1968 and was also available through the spares department under part number BD.29876 when replacements were required for earlier cars.

On the mechanical side quite significant changes were made to both cars. The 2.4 litre version received the straight port head as fitted to the E Type sports cars and for the first time on any 2.4 litre XK engine the Solex downdraught carburettors were replaced by twin HS6 1¾″ S.U.s, although retaining a manually operated choke from the lever control on the dashboard. Water circulation was improved with a full-flow system, and a new water-heated induction manifold was fitted, with the water rail built in instead of being an external part of the layout. A new wax thermostat was used which when opened blanked off the bypass and therefore ensured that circulation was entirely via the radiator. The distributor cap was also changed and now had side entry cables instead top entry. A new paper air-cleaner element replaced the previously used oil bath, with a cylinder type cleaner as opposed to the pancake type of the previous larger engined Mark IIs. The 'new' 2.4 litre engine followed Jaguar's trend to ribbed cam covers and to complete the engine modifications a new twin pipe exhaust system was standardised. The all synchromesh gearbox remained as before, with the alternative of the Borg Warner Type 35 automatic transmission.

These changes boosted power output to 133bhp at 5,500rpm compared with 120bhp at 5,750rpm, and increased torque to 146lb at 3,700rpm from 138lb at 3,000rpm, the majority of this increase in output coming from the installation of the straight port head. The 240 was now quicker than its predecessor and even quicker than the original 2.4 litre Mark I of 1956. With a

Ambla front seats replaced the Mark II's leather ones on the 240. They were similarly shaped but the number of stitched panels differed.

0 to 60mph time of 12.7 seconds and a top speed of well over 100mph the car was a true Jaguar performer. The 240 engine was much more flexible and powerful particularly at the top end of the rev. range. Helped by the lighter body the 240 could produce up to 25mpg.

All in all the 240 provided excellent value for money at a basic price of £1364, which was only £20 dearer than the very first 2.4 compact saloon of 1956 and was also cheaper than the previous Mark II version. With a production figure of 4450 the 240 was very popular with owners and road testers – yes, Jaguar actually let the 240 loose on motoring correspondents now that the car could beat the magical 100mph.

The larger engined car, the 340, was based on the previous 3,442cc XK engine but utilised the straight port head and other modifications as on the 240. Manual gearbox (with or without overdrive) was standard, with the Borg Warner Type 35 automatic transmission as an extra-cost option. The Marles Varamatic power steering system was also an extra cost option, available as before only on the larger engined cars. Exterior and internal changes were as on the 240 with the exception of the badging on the boot lid and radiator grille and the replacement of the 120mph speedometer with one calibrated to 140mph. The basic price of the 340 was £1422, again excellent value for money and cheaper than the old Mark II 3.4 litre version. Performance was again up on the equivalent Mark II, with a 0-60mph time of 8.8 seconds and a

maximum speed of some 124mph. The car could return a genuine 20mpg.

Despite rationalisation, both models were initially available in a variety of external colour finishes: Willow Green, British Racing Green, Signal Red, Regency Red (maroon), Old English White, Warwick Grey, Ascot Fawn, Sable, Indigo Blue and Primrose. By the end of production the colour range had been amended to include Light Blue (powder), Black, and White, with Signal Red being dropped. Interior colour schemes were very limited, only black, beige, green, dark blue or red being available. Optional extras at the time amounted to:

Heated Rear Window	**£18.00**
Overdrive	**£56.00**
Seat Belts	**£10.00**

plus radios, wire wheels, leather upholstery, special colour schemes, etc.

Perhaps the most unusual model produced at this time was the 380 – yes, Jaguar did produce a limited number of 3.8 litre 340s to special order. Nine cars were made between December 1967 and May 1968. All the cars concerned utilised the 3.8 litre S Type engine and were badged on the radiator grille 3.8 and on the boot lid 340 and 380! The model was never officially listed or publicised and it is not known what extra cost was involved. I am given to understand that the purchasers were customers who had previously had 3.8s. Again, no statistics are available but it is believed that all the cars concerned had leather upholstery and most a manual/overdrive gearbox.

As far as modifications to the 240/340 range were concerned, these were as diverse as the Mark IIs and covered the period from January 1968 to May 1969. In January of 1968 all Jaguars received a renewable petrol filter element, replacing the gauze type previously used. This took effect on the 240 from chassis numbers 1J.1429 (rhd) and 1J.30013 (lhd) and on the 340 from chassis numbers 1J.50480 (rhd) and 1J.80071 (lhd).

There was then a long gap until July of 1968, when numerous modifications were announced, starting with revised knock-on hub caps for wire wheeled cars destined for Denmark, Germany, Japan, Sweden or

Perhaps the ultimate model of the series, the Jaguar 380, complete with wire wheels, fog lamps, 3.8 litre engine, full synchromesh gearbox and leather upholstery.

Original factory badging for the 380 model.

Switzerland. A revised fitting and removal tool was also necessary and the modification commenced at chassis numbers 1J.1398 (240 rhd), 1J.30043 (240 lhd), 1J.50452 (340 rhd) and 1J.80094 (340 lhd). Again on export cars, from engine numbers 7J.2863 (240) and 7J.51686 (340) all cars bound for Canada had cylinder block heaters fitted as standard equipment and from the same engine number for the 240 and 7J.51712 (340), all cars were fitted with an improved crankshaft front oil seal, part number C.24611/1, and from chassis numbers 1J.30338 (240) and 1J.80286 (340) all cars destined for Germany had their side light bulbs integrated into the headlamps. The separate side lights remained in situ but were not wired up.

Moving on now to more conventional modifications, during July of 1968, at chassis numbers 1J.2037 (240 rhd), 1J.30225 (240 lhd), 1J.5118 (340 rhd) and 1J.80222 (340 lhd), Jaguar introduced a new water temperature gauge which had zonal dial markings, replacing the existing method of calibrating in degrees. The new gauge was marked NORMAL to indicate a safe water temperature, whilst the DANGER area was illustrated by means of red colouring. The same part was subsequently used as a spares replacement for all other models. From engine numbers 7J.2891 and 7J.51712 all cars had modified Lucas ignition coils with push-in teminals. At this time on the 340 (from engine number 7J.50001) revised struts for the oil suction and delivery pipes were fitted.

In December 1968, at chassis numbers 1J.30465 (240) and 1J.80425 (340), all left hand drive cars had the standard pattern LHD European headlamps (part no. C.21726) fitted replacing headlamp part number C.21728 which was for the Austrian market only. At chassis numbers 1J.3432 (240 rhd), 1J.30571 (240 lhd), 1J.52241 (340 rhd) and 1J.80536 (340 lhd) a new type of Lucas starter solenoid was fitted (part number C.30287). At the same chassis number on the 340 rhd and 1K.80535 (lhd) all 3.4 litre engined cars were fitted with an improved centre tie rod assembly incorporating modified ball end assemblies; this applied to cars fitted with power steering only. The new ball end assemblies were of steel/neoprene construction instead of the steel/rubber type previously used. In the same month all engines had sintered valve seat inserts fitted (part numbers C.28224 inlet and C.28225 exhaust) having reduced depth allowing for an improved valve seat pattern. On the 240 and 340 engines this modification took place from engine numbers 7J.3670 and 7J.52453 respectively. Finally, in December 1968 all engines were fitted with a modified (non-hydrostatic) clutch slave cylinder, replacing the previous hydrostatic model. Normal clutch wear was not automatically compensated for with this unit and any adjustment was to be made manually. This modification took effect from engine numbers 7J.3923 and 7J.52682 (240 and 340 respectively).

In January 1969 all engines received new connecting rod bolts (part number C.22246) and nuts (part number C.28535) with increased tensile strength. In March of that year an improved type of clutch unit, incorporating a higher rated diaphragm spring, was fitted. The new spring reduced the tendency towards clutch slip after a long period of service. This change affected 340 models only, from engine number 7J.52826. Around this time Jaguar had been informed of isolated cases of oil starvation in the overdrive unit on the all-synchromesh gearbox when cars were driven at high speed, due to a pumping action under certain condition. In March they therefore modified gearboxes in production by inserting a tapered expansion plug (part number C.16862/3) into the hole in the rear face of the gearbox and suggested to dealers that all other cars with the all-synchromesh gearbox should be duly modified.

In May 1969 a modified metallic petrol pipe assembly (filter to float chamber) was fitted to 240 models from engine number 7J.5358. At the same engine number a revised water pump spindle (part number C.8167/1) was fitted. During 1968 complaints had been received about stiff and sticking choke controls on lhd 240s and so Jaguar introduced a revised choke control cable comprising an acetal resin lined outer casing and a stranded inner cable.

One final modification was made in November 1971 affecting all Mark I, II and 240/340 cars concerning the supply of replacement bonnet mascots. Due to manufacturing difficulties in producing the old mascot (part number BD.10954), supplies were at that time no longer available and so Jaguar issued a replacement type (part number BD.29644) which varied from the original by the position of the mounting studs. The fitment of the new mascot necessitated the modification of both the rear centre chrome bead and front centre chrome bead by cutting back in length.

The 240 and 340 range had a relatively short life span, particularly the 340, of which only about 2,800 cars were produced, the last one in September 1968. The 240 soldiered on in production until April 1969 (left hand drive models terminating in March with a total production figure of only 535 units), the very last car rolling off the Browns Lane production line on 5th April. By this time the 240/340 models were beginning to look quite old fashioned when compared with modern machinery like the Rover and Triumph 2000s with their unrestricted vision, greater passenger area and, to some degee, extra refinement. With the advent of the Jaguar XJ6 in September 1968, the factory was looking to the seventies and eighties with an entirely new concept in saloon car manufacture, a one-model policy to satisfy all customer requirements.

As mentioned earlier the 240/340 models were often scorned as the cheapest and most undesirable of the whole compact Jaguar range, yet they were really underrated. The 240 was a fine car in its own right, with adequate performance and offering incredible value for money. The 340 was nearly as fast as an automatic-transmission 3.8 Mark II and again was excellent value in the over-3-litre bracket.

It is worth quoting the *Autocar* road test of the 240 saloon in January 1968, when they said, "Comparing figures with our test of the 2.4 on 21st September, 1956, one can see a big margin of improvement. Top speed is up from 102.5 to 106mph and almost 8 seconds are taken off the 0 to 80mph acceleration figures. Flexibility has not suffered at the expense of top end power, however. The 240 can still accelerate smoothly from 10 to 30mph in overdrive top in 12.7 seconds . . . The early 2.4 Mark I would run out of breath at 80mph and took a long run to reach maximum speed. The 240 spurts up to and cruises at 100mph in ease and with a lack of fuss . . ." I think this quote sums up the improvements made from 1956 to 1968, so perhaps the 240/340s were better cars than their predecessors and not just cheap and nasty variants! Unfortunately, throughout the whole production period of the Mark I and II, there was one area Jaguar could never master – the heating system! To quote again from the *Autocar* roadtest of the 240, "The one really dated aspect of the Jag is the heating, which can be left full on from the start of winter till the spring and hardly ever gets too hot."

With a grand total of over 128,730 Mark Is and IIs, 240s and 340s produced in thirteen years, the postwar compact Jaguar saloon deserves a prominent place in the history of Jaguar and of saloon cars in general.

Before closing this chapter on the 240/340 range, I would like to report on the cars from an owner's standpoint.

Graham Searle is membership secretary of the Jaguar Enthusiasts' Club and is the proud owner of a 1967 340 saloon in British Racing Green. It was 1977 when the bug bit and he decided he had to have a Jaguar. For Graham the only practical choice was a Mark II. Having little knowledge of the model and with limited resources, he scoured the local papers. The only thing in his price range was a 340 – cheap, attainable and above all a Jaguar – so he bought it!

Initially, at club events, Graham was made to feel a little regretful as most Mark II owners took great delight in informing him that his 340 was not a 'proper' Jaguar. However, after a body rebuild and various mechanical changes, Graham still owns OYB 593F and is very proud of her. In Graham's own words, "It is a Jaguar and therefore the ride and power are unquestioned. The straight port head developed for the 240, coupled with the lighter bodyshell, make it a very fast car indeed, even by modern standards."

Graham's car has the standard Ambla upholstery, a feature which Graham finds beneficial with two young children, as he thinks the Ambla finish takes the wear much better. It is also considerably cheaper to replace. When this particular car left the factory it was a basic model, not even equipped with overdrive. Graham has now fitted overdrive and changed the rear axle ratio from 3.77 to 3.54. The car now loses out slightly on acceleration but gains very much on fuel economy, easily attaining 26mpg on a run. Graham also finds his 340 a great tow-car – "With the caravan behind I have to remind myself it's there! The-all synchro box coupled with the seemingly limitless torque make towing a pleasure, and on long weekends away it means the whole family can make maximum use of the car, but I can still return 20 plus miles per gallon when towing." OYB is shod with radial tyres, a feature that Graham thinks suits these later models better than the earlier Mark IIs.

For a further owner's view I spoke to Mr P.H. Hammond, the very fortunate owner of the only known surviving 380 saloon, finished in Regency Red with beige interior and registered TMM 451F. Mr. Hammond bought the car through Hexagon Motors, I don't think realising the true significance of his purchase at first. As mentioned earlier, only nine of this rare breed were ever built by Jaguar to special customer orders. This particular car has all the trimmings: leather upholstery, sun-roof, manual/overdrive gearbox and wire wheels, although this last item was fitted after leaving the factory.

The 380 left the Jaguar factory on the 18th March 1968 with the very unusual engine number SE 2011-8, not a suffix used on either 340 or 3.8 litre Mark II engines but now believed to be an S Type unit. Mr Hammond has himself tried hard to trace the history of this and other 380s with little success. No mention of the 380 is made in Jaguar's records, which further complicates matters. If anyone has any knowledge of these cars or even knows the whereabouts of them today, Mr Hammond can be contacted through the author.

TMM 451F is now in magnificent (almost concours) condition and Mr Hammond is justly proud of her. He claims the car is exceptionally quick even by 3.8 Mark II standards, has tremendous torque and is particularly smooth on the open road. He is convinced that his 380 is the ultimate Mark II and I think I am inclined to agree with him.

Graham Searle with his 340.

A 240 in standard form.

A Jaguar by another name!

Daimler was one of the pioneering names in the motor industry and had traditionally built quality, prestige cars for the carriage trade. After the Second World War, Daimler started to produce 'standard steel' saloons for the upper-middle-class market and some of these cars did compete in the same market place as Jaguar. In the fifties the Daimler Conquest and Conquest Century were Daimler's answer to the compact Jaguar and in the late fifties and early sixties their Majestic Major was an out and out rival to the Mark IX Jaguar (and in fact could outperform the Jaguar by a handsome margin). Daimler, however, had lost a lot of ground to Jaguar, never being able to offer the same value for money or be as fashionable as the 'cats' from Browns Lane.

With the general decline in the carriage trade Daimler looked elsewhere to replace lost sales. In 1959 they introduced a rather unusual sports car with a glass-fibre body known as the SP250. Although this car does not directly concern us here, it is significant in that it embodied a previously unused V8 engine designed by Edward Turner, more famous for his motorcycle engineering achievements. Daimler had planned to use this new power unit in a saloon, but not having the time or finance to design their own new car, considered using an existing model from one of the mass-producers to suitably "Daimlerise". The car they chose to upgrade to Daimler standards of luxury was the Vauxhall Cresta, which would have been modified with a Daimler fluted radiator grille, more shapely panels and a revised interior using leather and fine veneers. In the end nothing came of the project (perhaps thankfully!) and Daimler entered the sixties with only two standard production models, the SP250 sports car and the big Majestic Major saloon. Neither car was built in sufficient quantities to help Daimler's ailing market position.

In May of 1960 it was announced that Jaguar Cars Limited had purchased the assets of the Daimler concern for a modest £3.4 million, which was extremely beneficial to Jaguar as this gave them access to extra manufacturing facilities at Daimler's Radford-based factory, extra space that was urgently needed and in fact literally doubled Jaguar's production capacity. Initially, production of Daimler cars continued unchanged, the SP250 not being in direct competition with the XK sports car, and although the Majestic was competitive against Jaguar's Mark IX, it was not produced in sufficient quantities to threaten sales of the big Jaguar.

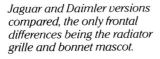

Jaguar and Daimler versions compared, the only frontal differences being the radiator grille and bonnet mascot.

Jaguar engineers were very enthusiastic about the Daimler 2.5 litre V8 power unit used in the SP250 and experimented with the idea of using the engine in a Jaguar designed saloon. Initial trials were carried out using a works 'hack' Mark I Jaguar with the standard SP250 power unit installed. The results were apparently very encouraging – so much so that plans were made to install the V8 in the Mark II Jaguar shell to form the basis of a new upmarket Daimler version of the range. It was never planned that the Daimler should replace any of the Mark II variants but that it should develop a market position of its own, a market still maintained today with the current Daimler (Jaguar based) derivatives.

The lightweight V8 engine had a bore and stroke of 76.2mm x 69.85mm and a cubic capacity of 2,548cc. It developed 140bhp at 5,800rpm, with a maximum torque of 155lb at 3,000rpm. The cylinder block was cast iron, with two interchangeable aluminium heads. The valves were operated by pushrods from a single camshaft. The camshaft itself was centrally mounted, high in the block between the V. The engine operated at a compression ratio of 8.2 to 1. Twin 1¾" HD6 SU carburettors were fitted, with a manually operated choke mechanism. Certain modifications had to be made to the engine to allow insertion into the Mark II shell, which included revised head fixing bolts to enable the heads to be removed with the engine in situ, a new sump in order to clear the Mark II subframe crossmembers, and a repositioned water pump.

The 90° V8 sat well down in the engine compartment but the plugs were ideally placed for servicing, as were the carburettors, air filter, power steering unit and reservoirs. Although the engine was built mostly of aluminium alloys, it was by no means noisy, in fact quite the opposite, and although it was a comparatively high revving unit (an unusual feature in a luxury saloon car), it was exceptionally smooth throughout the rev. range. New exhaust manifolds were used with down pipes allowing the necessary clearance in the tight engine bay, leading to a twin exhaust system running the full length of the underside on either side, emerging at the rear at the furthermost extremities of the body's width. A conventional Borg Warner Type 35 automatic transmission was used but, unlike on the Jaguars, this unit had no facility for an intermediate speed hold. A manual gearbox was not initially available on the Daimler as it was envisaged that the type of person buying the model would not normally require the option. As the V8 engine was substantially lighter than the Mark II unit, there was less weight over the front wheels and therefore spring ratings were altered and the dampers set much softer.

External changes to the Mark II bodyshell were very subtle, with the fitting of a well designed traditional Daimler fluted radiator grille, a very neat Daimler

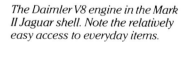

The Daimler V8 engine in the Mark II Jaguar shell. Note the relatively easy access to everyday items.

Rear end differences include ribbed number plate light housing and badging. The 'disc brake' badge on the rear bumper was replaced by a 'D' insignia on the Daimlers.

'D' mascot on the leading edge of the bonnet and a much thicker (triangular section) centre bonnet chrome strip similar to that used on the Mark X models completing the frontal modifications. The Daimler flutes were continued at the rear of the car, with the numberplate nacelle redesigned to match the radiator grille. The traditional 'D' motif featured on a badge adorning the centre of the rear bumper (replacing the 'Disc Brake' sign on Mark IIs). Daimler script was used on the boot lid, with other badges stating 'V8' and 'Automatic' occupying the space at the bottom of the lid. The 'D' insignia was further used in the centre of the hub-caps (which were of the same design as Jaguar) and for the first time on any compact model from Browns Lane Rimbellishers were supplied as standard equipment. In all other aspects the exterior of the new Daimler was exactly as a Jaguar. On the road the Daimler was instantly recognisable by the radiator grille at the front and the two chrome-trimmed exhaust pipes emerging from either side at the rear, and if both these pointers missed one's keen eye there was always the unmistakable throb of the V8 power unit to differentiate the Daimler from a Jaguar.

Internal changes were a little more noticeable, the main instantly recognisable pointer being the lack of a centrally mounted transmission tunnel. The normal Jaguar console was dispensed with, allowing the use of a split bench type seat arrangement for the front seats, with large cushions each 20″ deep and 26″ wide; this seating arrangement was a throwback to the Mark I days when a similar set-up was adopted. With no floor mounted gearlever it gave an extra front seat passenger ample room. Alternatively, centre fold-away armrests were provided to 'split' the seating arrangement, affording more lateral support. Front seats were still individually adjustable for fore and aft movement. The front seat backs were much slimmer and did not accommodate picnic tables, nor did the interior boast heater ducts for the rear seat passengers, there being no provision for the pipes from the heating system. There was, however, slightly more legroom for rear seat passengers.

The dashboard remained exactly as on the Mark II except that the radio, heater controls and ashtray were now slung underneath the centre map pocket. Although finished in matching wood veneer this unit nevertheless looked a little 'added on'. The ashtray was of a simple pull-out type used on many Rootes Group cars of the period. The steering wheel, the same design as

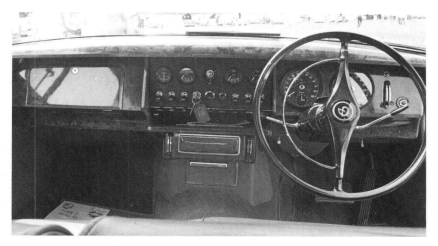

Dashboard changes for the Daimler included a 'D' insignia to the steering wheel, and the radio mounting, heater controls and ashtray hung from the centre parcel shelf.

on Mark IIs, sported the 'D' insignia (gold on black) in the centre boss and the speedometer was only calibrated to a maximum of 120mph. The interior woodwork on Daimlers always seemed of a slightly better standard than the Jaguars' with more figuring to the veneers and a deeper look. The only other internal change involved the headlining and interior courtesy lights, the former differing in that it was 'sprung' into position and the latter in that there were only three light fittings (one above the rear window in the centre, and one on each centre pillar) instead of four.

The new compact Daimler was released to the public in October 1962 as the 2.5 V8, and the initial purchase price was £1,568.19s.7d. including purchase tax. Optional extras at that time included power assisted steering at £66.9s.2d., reclining front seat mechanisms at £16.6s.3d. and the other usual Jaguar type options of radio, wire wheels, etc. A heated rear window was supposedly an optional extra but to my knowledge all cars were fitted with one before leaving the factory. Exterior paint finishes were initially as the Mark II Jaguars although on the cars produced there was a strong leaning towards the metallic range, particularly opalescent blue, silver and gunmetal.

The 2.5 V8 ("Daimler-Jag" as it affectionately became known, or "crinkle-cut Jag" unaffectionately) was quite a significant car in the history of Jaguar. It was the only Daimler to be produced by the company utilising a non-Jaguar power unit, which must say a lot for the design of the V8. At the price, the car was pitched at a market not directly coinciding with the buyers of the Mark II range; it was generally felt that with the demise of the true Daimler compacts, there was an empty 'niche' for a slightly upmarket version of the Jaguar to suit the more stately type of driver. Jaguar were right in assuming the 2.5 would fit the bill.

The new Daimler performed exceptionally well and actually proved to be faster, quieter and smoother than its Jaguar counterpart, the 2.4 litre Mark II. With a 0 to 60mph time of 13.2 seconds and a top speed of 112mph (although at much higher revs because of the low axle ratio of 4.55) the car was certainly no sluggard. Road-test acceleration times were:

0 to 30mph	**4.6 seconds**
0 to 40mph	**6.8 seconds**
0 to 50mph	**9.6 seconds**
0 to 60mph	**13.2 seconds**
0 to 70mph	**18.0 seconds**
0 to 80mph	**23.6 seconds**
0 to 90mph	**31.2 seconds**

Although the engine was only of 2½ litres capacity, fuel consumption suffered somewhat against the 2.4 Jaguar, with a figure of only 17mpg, but in all other respects the Daimler was a match for the smaller engined Jaguar and immediately found support from the Daimler clientele. One further advantage the Daimler could boast over its sister Jaguar, not instantly recognisable unless one had driven both cars, was that the steering was lighter. With less engine weight, steering was much more acceptable even without power assistance.

The 2.5 V8 received notable acclaim from journalists and owners alike. The particularly smooth engine was almost inaudible at tick-over and gave a typically V8 'throb' under acceleration. *Sportscar* magazine, when testing the Daimler in 1963, said, "A successful marriage of a smooth, free-revving V8 engine and lightweight but robust automatic transmission to the structure of a very popular high-performance four/five seater saloon". The Daimler was very much a British product for a British market and was never exported to the North American market, where the Daimler name did not have the same significance as Jaguar. In fact hardly any V8s were produced with left-hand drive.

As far as modifications during production are concerned, most of the alterations covered previously in the Mark II chapters are applicable, particularly in relation to the chassis and suspension. Other known modifications specific to the Daimler included the following. In January 1964 the rear axle ratio was altered to 4.27 (from 4.55) giving slightly improved economy (around 19mpg) but at the expense of acceleration. In April 1964 the Borg Warner automatic transmission was modified to incorporate D1 and D2 settings, making the whole car more flexible and giving smoother gear changes. Manual gearbox options (from the Jaguar 2.4) became available from February 1967 but were rarely supplied with an overdrive unit, for some reason, and at the same time the engine mountings were strengthened. After 1965 a limited slip differential became an optional extra.

Major changes were made to the Daimler in September 1967, one week after the launch of the Jaguar 240/340 range. The changes basically revolved around the same theme as the Jaguar's, with economy measures being introduced. The most noticeable was the fitment of slim-line bumpers front and rear with matching over-riders, modified valances and hub-caps exactly as on the Jaguars. The Daimler fluted trim was retained, and as a token of respect for this upmarket Mark II, the fog lamps remained a standard fitment on Daimlers as did wheel Rimbellishers.

As far as the interior was concerned, reclining seats were now standardised and the dashboard, although substantially unaltered, now boasted a padded roll to the top windscreen rail, only available in black regardless of interior trim colour, and of a Rexine material. Referring to *Sportscar* magazine of 1963 again, "The wood screen rail provided reflections in the lower part of the front windscreen – a matt black top covering could be more beneficial". Perhaps Jaguar actually took notice of this road-tester's comments but it is difficult to understand why the padded roll was not added to the Jaguar versions. I do know of one 240 which has this feature but am not convinced it was fitted by the factory. The padding was continued on Daimlers to include the door cappings in a similar fashion to the 420 Jaguar saloons. Leather seating continued as a standard fitment on Daimlers (optional at extra cost on Jaguars) but new style ventilated panels were used.

Mechanically the Daimler now utilised the Marles Varamatic power steering system, replacing the previous type, and an alternator was standardised. Pistons were modified shortly after production of the revised model (now designated V8 250) and separate air cleaners, one for each carburettor, were fitted, improving access generally to the engine area.

Prices for the V8 250 model started at £1,613 for a manual gearbox car without overdrive, £1,660 for the manual with overdrive option and £1,698 for the automatic transmission version.

Split bench seating with centre arm-rests replaced the bucket type of the Mark II. The central transmission tunnel was much smaller. Slight differences to the interior door trims should also be noted.

Back seats as in the Jaguars but again note the slight difference in rear door trim panels.

Exterior colour schemes had been modified in line with the Jaguar range although metallics were still predominant and opalescent Silver Blue, Silver and Maroon were still available as standard colours. British Racing Green, Sable and Old English White were amongst the other most popular colour options for Daimlers.

Autosport magazine road-tested a manual/overdrive version of the V8 250 on the 18th October 1968 and found the car a distinct improvement over the previous automatic model. Similar top speeds were recorded but with an extra 1,000rpm in hand. They also found the handling slightly better than on the equivalent Jaguar. Comment was passed that the V8 engine did not have a lot of punch at low speeds but was exceptionally smooth and would crawl and idle in traffic indefinitely. They went on to say that the engine was never noisy but that they found the fuel consumption a little disappointing at less than 20mpg. They concluded, "The Daimler V8 250 is a dignified carriage with an engine of sporting type. Now that it is available with a manual gearbox, the owner can enjoy the sporting side of its character without prejudice to its more stately virtues."

Production of the Daimler V8 250 was terminated in July 1969 when a total of 8,880 cars had been produced. A limited production run by any mass-produced standards, but the Daimler commanded a loyalty totally distinct from the Jaguar image and judging by the prices today these cars are fast appreciating and therefore maintaining their status. The demise of the V8 250 came about for two reasons. Firstly, as with the 240/340 Jaguars, the car was by then a little long in the tooth; and secondly, the other Jaguar-based Daimlers (the 420 Sovereign and XJ Sovereign) had taken the limelight.

In order to get some reaction from a typical Daimler owner I spoke to Mr Samuel Barnes, a Daimler V8 owner since 1967. His car is a V8 250 bought new in 1967, an automatic transmission version finished in opalescent Silver Grey with dark grey interior. Mr Barnes used to cover on average 200 miles per week in his Daimler as a businessman, with additional long business trips out of town, and holiday motoring, and the car has now covered a grand total of around 85,000 miles entirely in his hands.

Mr Barnes had previously run a 2.4 litre Jaguar and was attracted to the Daimler derivative because of the extra comfort and the particularly smooth engine. After the Jaguar he found the Daimler a quieter, more appealing car. He particularly likes the automatic transmission as this suits the style of the Daimler. Having driven many different types of motor car before the Daimler and since, Mr Barnes still feels his V8 is superior in many ways. Not a fast driver, he has regularly achieved exceptionally good fuel consumption – 25/27mpg on a long run.

Mr Barnes states that his Daimler has been truly 100% reliable, needing no major work of any kind either mechanically or bodily. The only untoward incident involved the brake reservoir tank under the offside front wing, which rotted through in 1983. Otherwise the bodywork and interior are still in immaculate condition and the engine as quiet as ever. As Mr Barnes is now retired, the car is not used during the winter months, but it is still used extensively during the summer and he has no plans to part with it.

The Daimler V8-250 saloon. As with the Jaguar 240, note the thinner bumpers and new hub-caps, although fog-lights and wheel trims remain a standard fitment on the Daimlers.

The Mark II in Competition

During the early years of production the Mark IIs were synonymous with competition. 3.8s in particular were virtually unbeatable in touring car races from 1960 to 1963, becoming a legend in their own time. No other Jaguar saloon before or since that time has had such success, or ever won such overwhelming acceptance from competitors and spectators alike. A lot of this success can be put down to the phenomenal reliability of the cars – it has been said to me by one mechanic from those days, "going to the circuits with the Mark IIs was like a holiday". The sight and sound of a Mark II on full bore round a corner with one wheel in the air and the sill almost touching the ground must have stirred the adrenalin – and remember that a 3.8 litre in full race trim could produce up to 280bhp, making it a potent machine by any standards. The cars competed in so many events during the sixties that it is an impossible task to list and comment on every one. To do so would fill a whole book, and such a task is best left to specialists on Jaguar's competition history like Andrew Whyte. The following is therefore a brief resumé of some of the Mark II's competitive activities up to the present day, and I trust will stand as a tribute to the design and engineering of these fine cars.

The very first car modified for competition by the factory was a 3.4 litre delivered in 1960 to David MacKay for racing in his home country of Australia, where he had up to that time successfully campaigned a Mark I. Many famous Mark IIs followed, including BUY 12, a 3.8 litre modified by John Coombs which was still racing in the 1970s in the capable hands of Tony Strawson. The most competitive Mark IIs were, of course, the 3.8s. The John Coombs organisation modified several cars for racing and amongst their famous drivers was Roy Salvadori, always a star performer, who won most of his races in 1960 with a Mark II. Other famous Mark II drivers included Sir Gawaine Baillie, Peter Jopp, Bruce McLaren and John Surtees. Never was a saloon so widely campaigned by so many star drivers.

The Mark II seemed indestructible: a good example of this is the ex-factory car 1628 VC, built in October 1960 supposedly to be run to destruction by the experimental department at Browns Lane. Roy Salvadori drove this car, followed by John Sparrow, until 1965. Later in its life 1628 VC was fitted with a 7 litre Chevrolet engine and was subsequently used for drag racing. The car survives to this day in the hands of avid competition supporter and Mark II fanatic Tim Spital, and perhaps one day it will race again.

One of the most remarkable Mark IIs, 1628 VC, which still survives to this day.

A typical saloon car race at Goodwood during the early sixties.

Although the 3.8 was the competitive version of the Mark II, 3.4s were seen occasionally on the track and in rallies, and even the odd 2.4 litre car turned out, one of which was the car driven by Chris Kerrison, who competed in numerous events with some degree of success in the smaller engined classes. Many cars for competition were modified in a similar fashion to Mark Is. Later Mark IIs were further modified with reinforced suspension, alloy panels, wider rear wheels and extensively modified engines, sometimes with triple carburettors, etc.

1960 saw the start of the famous Mark II domination and the cars were campaigned in all types of competitive motor sport. At the Easter Monday Goodwood meeting of that year Mark IIs were driven by Roy Salvadori and Jack Sears, and although putting up a good fight were unfortunately beaten into first place by Stirling Moss in an Aston Martin. Later, at the Snetterton circuit, Sir Gawaine Baillie in his privately entered 3.8 (registered GB 448) redressed the balance by attaining the first outright win for the Mark II. In the Lancashire and Cheshire Car Club's national meeting at Oulton Park in 1960, Baillie again finished first at 75.81mph, with R. Harris second and Ian Hodgson third, all in 3.8s, in the over 3,000cc class. During the British Grand Prix meeting at Silverstone in July, Jack Sears, Sir Gawaine Baillie, Dennis Taylor and John Surtees, as well as Colin Chapman (of Lotus fame), competed in 3.8s, with Bill Aston and Kennerly in 3.4s. Chapman, Surtees, Sears and Baillie made up the front row of the grid and after seven laps Chapman (6 PPF) got past Sears (in the Tommy Sopwith car JAG 400) by using most of the grass verge instead of the circuit – Mark IIs seemed to have this effect on some drivers. Again and again the cars changed places, with Chapman finally winning by only 0.2 seconds on the last lap in his John Coombs modified car. According to contemporary reports on the event the Jaguar drivers drove as though the devil were behind them, giving a spectacular display for the spectators. At the same venue, in the Production Car event, which had been won by Jaguar ever since the race was inaugurated, the Mark IIs had stiff competition from Dan Gurney in his huge Chevrolet Impala. Jaguar, however, won again with Graham Hill first, followed by Parkes in the by now well known JAG 400, and Bruce McLaren third, all in 3.8s. The American invasion was to be thwarted, at least for the time being. Going back to May 1960, and again at Silverstone, Mark IIs took the first four places, producing a Jaguar walkover in the International Trophy Race. Roy Salvadori took first place in his Coombs car, followed by Stirling Moss in an Equipe Endeavour car and Graham Hill in third place with a Team Speedwell 3.8. Sir Gawaine Ballie took fourth place in his privately entered 3.8. In the same month Baillie also competed at Aintree, finishing a creditable third, and at Brands Hatch Baillie's old 3.4 Mark I competed in the hands of Bill Aston, beaten unfortunately by Powell in another of the new 3.8s.

On the rally scene in 1960 the Mark II was also proving a force to be reckoned with. In the Alpine Rally Jose Behra and René Richard won the Touring Car Class and Coupe des Alpes in a 3.8 Mark II, with Parkes and Geoff Howarth in another 3.8 taking third and fifth overall. In the Tour de France Bernard Consten and Jacques Renal won their class (although by a small margin) from the other 3.8 of Peter Jopp and Sir Gawaine Baillie. The *Autocar* report of 21st October 1960 commented, "What excellent value the new Jaguar models represent. The recent Tour de France in which they won the touring class saw virtually standard models lapping the Spa and Le Mans cicuits at more than 100mph."

In the Monte Carlo Rally of the same year Walter and Brinkman did not do that well in their 3.8, although they did manage to win one of the hill-climb sections. In the Tulip Rally, however, Boardman and Whitworth won their class with a 3.8 and made 11th overall, with Parkes and Gatsonides competing in another Mark II (registered 1370HP, actually the 80th car produced). In the R.A.C. Rally of November 1960 Jack Sears and Willy Cave came fourth in their 3.8, also winning their class. An excellent start to the rallying career of the Mark II saloon.

1960 had proved an excellent year for the Mark II and Jaguar were not to be disappointed with 1961. At the May Silverstone meeting McLaren, Surtees and Dennis Taylor competed in 3.8s along with Salvadori in his Coombs car and Parkes and Hill in a Sopwith car. Hill subsequently won, breaking the touring car lap record at 92.11mph and urged on to victory by a Chevrolet hot on his heels. 1961 also saw the first ever endurance race held at the Nürburgring. Jaguar's German dealer Peter Lindner with his co-driver Peter Nocker put up a fine effort in a 3.4, winning despite savage clutch problems. This proved the first major win for the 3.4. At the Lombard Trophy meeting at Snetterton Jack Sears and Mike Parkes were leading in their 3.8 but ran out of petrol on the last lap, allowing privateer Sir Gawaine Baillie to win in his Mark II. In the Circuit of Ireland race Bobby Parkes in another 3.8 with John Cuff in a 3.4 each won their respective classes, and on the other side of the world in Australia Robert Jane appeared in his 3.8 at Queensland but had to retire through the failure of a rear spring.

In the 1961 Alpine Rally Sir Gawaine Baillie and Peter Jopp won their class in a 3.8, and in the Tour de France Bernard Consten again won his class, with Rossinski, Richard and André Chollet taking second, third and fourth places, all in Jaguars. Mark IIs continued to enter the Monte Carlo Rally, although again with little success, Eric Brinkman and Philip Walton finishing

Graham Hill at the wheel of the Coombs BUY 12 at Goodwood in 1962.

104th and 130th respectively. The R.A.C. Rally also proved a little 'rough' for the compact Jaguars but nevertheless John Casewell entered and finished a very creditable 49th in his 3.8, registered NBF 955. Chris Kerrison continued to campaign his 2.4 litre Mark II with some limited success.

For the 1962 season Graham Hill and Roy Salvadori signed on for the John Coombs team again, and Jack Sears and Bobby Parkes for the rival Equipe Endeavour team. David Hobbs and Sir Gawaine Baillie continued as private entrants for all events. At the British Grand Prix meeting at Aintree the Australian Bob Jane led Bobby Parkes and Jack Sears, all in Mark IIs. Jane unfortunately later retired through overheating but not until he had made the fastest lap of the race. Bob Jane, incidentally, made quite a name for himself, with no less than 48 firsts in his home country from 1962 to 1963. At Brands Hatch in May, Jaguars driven by Dodds, Baillie and Salvadori competed, only to be beaten to first place by a Chevrolet Impala driven by Kelsey. Jaguar managed second, third and fourth places (Salvadori, Baillie and Dodds), Salvadori taking the lap record. At Crystal Palace in June Roy Salvadori again competed in the famous Coombs car BUY 12 with other Mark IIs entered by Sears and Baillie, all of them occupying the front row of the grid. Although this race saw the further intervention of the big American cars into the English competitive scene, Salvadori managed to take first place, with Sears second and Baillie fourth. At the Whitsun national meeting at Castle Combe John Sparrow took first place overall in his newly acquired ex-factory 3.8 (1628 VC).

In the Oulton Park Trophy Race Salvadori competed again in BUY 12 along with Sears, Dodd and Baillie, Baillie finishing fourth in his usual GB 448, the other Jaguars losing out to the Americans. At the B.R.S.C.C.-organised six hour endurance race at Brands Hatch, sponsored by the *Motor* (this was the first long distance saloon car event in this country), 3.8s again hit the headlines, Mike Parkes and Jimmy Blummer winning, with Lindner and Nocker second (this time in a 3.8 as opposed to their 3.4).

Abroad too Mark IIs were again showing their worth in 1962. In the Buenos Aires Production Car Race, a 500-mile event, Rodriguez Larretta and Jack Greene won after no less than twenty-five wheel changes, highlighting the continual tyre trouble experienced with the Mark IIs. In many cases one set of tyres would just about last one race! Other Jaguars entered the race, one finishing fifth and the other meeting with engine failure. In the Kyalami Nine Hour race in South Africa Ian Fraser-Jones and Chris Griffith got sixth overall and won on handicap in their 3.8. In the Touring Car six hour endurance event at the Nürburging Lindner led all the way in his 3.8, finishing over half a lap ahead of the second placed car (a Lancia) and averaging over 70mph. Jaguars took first, third and fifth placings and were awarded the team prize. A fourth Jaguar driven by Schodrach unfortunately retired but at one time was holding second place. In the twelve hour endurance event Peter Lindner and J. Walter also won for Jaguar.

Rally events again proved successful for the Mark II in 1962. In the Tour de France Jaguar dominated the touring car category for the fourth year, 3.8s taking the first five places in their class. No less than ten 3.8s were entered (five of which were private entries). At the start Bernard Consten tried to convince everyone that the 2″ carburettors and extra fuel tanks on the Lego/Sears and Jopp/Baillie cars had not been homologated, unconvincingly! The event commenced at Rouen on 16th September with 73 cars in the touring car category (including the ten Jaguars). The Sears red car collided with a Citröen while overtaking, leaving the road. Sears suffered back injuries which put him in hospital and of course out of the race. Just after this Baillie's car left the road plunging down a 100 foot drop. In the end first place went to Consten for the third year running (despite his concern over the carburettor size of the other Jaguars). In the Monte Carlo Rally Walter and Robson came 118th, which was not a particularly good result, this rally never seeming to suit the Mark II.

For 1963 the big event was the European Touring Car Championship and the first round was held at the Nürburgring circuit as a six hour endurance event. Mercedes fielded a full works team in an attempt to beat the Jaguar entrants led by Peter Lindner and co-driver Peter Nocker in a Group 2 factory prepared 3.8. Lindner's car took pole position on the grid and maintained a small lead from the start. A Mercedes followed hot on the heels of the Jaguar until it took an unscheduled pit-stop, which gave Lindner the chance to leap ahead and win the race. During the 1963 season the Jaguar remained on maximum points, giving Lindner first place in the E.T.C. championship. Amongst the other Jaguars competing in the E.T.C. championship was John Sparrow's 1628 VC, which retired at the Nürburgring with a broken drive-shaft but which managed to take second place at Zandvoort.

One of the most famous Mark II photographs of them all, showing the Lindner-Nocker Mark II.

The other, perhaps most memorable and certainly best publicised Mark II event of 1963 took place at the Monza circuit on 6th March, when former motorcycle champion Geoff Duke led a team of drivers consisting of John Bekaert, Andrew Hedges, Peter Lumsden and Peter Sargeant in a four day marathon of record breaking, averaging 105mph and taking no less than four international records for the Mark II saloon. The International Class C (3,000 to 5,000cc) awards were:-

10,000 miles	**106.58mph**
15,000 km	**106.61mph**
Three days	**107.02mph**
Four days	**106.62mph**

Jaguar had previously held these records with another of their models, an XK120 driven by Leslie Johnson and Stirling Moss at Montlhéry in 1952. For this 1963 marathon Jaguar used a 3.8 registered 7116 VC, opalescent silver grey in colour, which had had a number of modifications carried out to help with reliability and ease of maintenance. Externally the car was equipped with a third windscreen wiper (fitted on the roof), twin Lucas Flamethrower spotlights, wire wheels and Dunlop racing tyres, an external bonnet release catch, and the overriders and rear wheel spats had been removed. Internally the car was standard except for much modified competition seating for both driver and front seat passenger and the removal of the transmission tunnel, heater, ducts, etc. A small addition was a sign posted in front of the driver saying "No matter what happens, bring it back to the pits".

Mechanically, quite a number of changes were made, the most significant of which was a change of rear axle ratio from 3.77 to 2.93. This gave an unbelievable 36mph per 1000rpm with a conventional overdrive car but in this case the overdrive had been deliberately locked out, thus allowing a genuine 100mph at 3,500rpm. Although overdrive would have been permissible under the regulations, Jaguar did not want to take the risk of a mechanical or electrical failure affecting the final results of the run. The pancake air filter was replaced by a pair of trumpet inlets direct into the carburettors, a secondary coil was fitted alongside the standard one, and a competition exhaust and high ratio steering box were employed. An auxiliary fuel tank giving a total capacity of 39 gallons was fitted in the boot (with separate external filler) and a host of spare parts and an extra spare wheel had to be carried.

The run started on Wednesday 6th March as an attempt at the seven day record, but on Friday 8th March the record had to be abandoned when the car's back axle fractured near the Panhard rod link, this breakage caused apparently by the axle hitting the chassis as the car came off the Monza banking. By Saturday a new axle had been fitted and the car returned to the circuit in the hands of Peter Lumsden. Despite rain, mist and the atrocious road surface the car completed 2,500 miles in the first twenty-four hours and after forty-eight hours 5,117 miles. The drivers took three-hour stints at the wheel with scheduled pit stops. There were further problems on the Wednesday morning when one of the petrol tanks split. The car continued with a greatly reduced fuel load, which necessitated refuelling every hour. Despite this the set averages were maintained, and by 8.10pm on Wednesday evening 10,000 miles had been covered.

The Mark II had used up no less than four front and fourteen rear tyres, but had averaged 14mpg of fuel and 480 miles per pint of oil. The event was a success for Jaguar and for the reputation of the Mark II. The marathon was exceptionally well publicised through all the national motoring magazines and at the Motor Show of that year Jaguar exhibited their prize endurance car.

Returning now to the more conventional competition activities of the Mark IIs in 1963, in April at Oulton Park Bill Aston, Mike Salmon, Graham Hill

Mark II at speed at Monza on its record-breaking run.

and Roy Salvadori competed. Graham Hill finished in first place with the other Mark IIs taking second and third. At the International Easter Goodwood meeting Salvadori, Hill and Salmon competed together again, with Hill (in his Coombs car) winning, Mark IIs also taking the next five places – domination indeed! John Sparrow actually took second place in his old workhorse 1628 VC, and the same weekend at the Silverstone event he managed first place, followed by second place the next day at Mallory Park – quite a weekend! At the Whitsun Goodwood meeting Mike Salmon won in his ex-Coombs 3.8. Unfortunately, at the August Bank Holiday meeting at Brands Hatch, Jaguar were to lose out to the ever increasing challenge of the big American machines, this time in the shape of Ford Galaxies. Graham Hill came second, however, in his 3.8, pipped to first place by Jim Clark. At Silverstone in May Roy Salvadori came second at 90.38mph to Jack Sears in a 7 litre Galaxie.

Another well-known Coombs Mark II from the sixties, this time 4578NK, at Brands Hatch.

For the Brands Hatch six hour race Lindner and Nocker again competed, only to be disqualified for an oversized inlet manifold. The race was nevertheless won by Roy Salvadori and Denny Hulme in another 3.8, also managing to take the fastest lap. Old faithful 1628 VC also competed but was unplaced. Despite the increasing threat from across the water Jaguar still had some wins to come, with Salvadori winning the Lombard Touring Car Race at Snetterton and Lindner/Nocker winning the Nürburgring 12 hour race again in July (although only by a matter of two seconds). On this occasion Lindner broke the lap record at 80.77mph. Other British and European successes for the Mark II at that time included a first for Graham Hill in the Aintree 200 race, and firsts for Peter Lindner and Peter Nocker in the Hockenheim Touring Car race, the German Grand Prix meeting and the Grand Prix meeting at Zolder.

On the rally scene for 1963, in the Tour de France Bernard Consten/ Jacques Renal won again, marking Jaguar's fifth successive victory in the touring car category, with Annie Soisbault and Louisette Texier second, both in Mark IIs. Sir Gawaine Baillie and Peter Jopp had by this time abandoned Jaguar in favour of the vast Galaxies. In the Tulip Rally Lundberg and Lindstrom in a 3.8 came second in their class, with John Sprinzel and Barry Hughes third (in HJK 380). This was the first and only time John Sprinzel drove a Jaguar in a rally. Jaguar's Australian ally Bob Jane kept up the tradition in his

The J. Dunster Coombs-modified Mark II cornering on the limit at Goodwood in September 1967.

modified 3.8 by winning no less than 38 races in succession. This particular car had three Weber carburettors, special manifold, camshafts, sump, oil cooler, suspension and braking system and could produce well over 300bhp. Some of his 1963 successes included firsts in the Australian Grand Prix meeting, Lakeside Touring Car Race, South Pacific Gold Star meeting, Australian R.A.C. TT meeting, Victoria Touring championship, Sandown Park, and the New South Wales Touring Championship at Katoomba. In New Zealand things were also going well for the Mark II, with Tony Shelly and Ray Archibold winning the Wills 6 hour race, Ray also taking first place in the Lady Wigran Trophy meeting and Alistair McBeath making first place at the New Zealand Grand Prix meeting. In another part of the world South African Fraser Jones won the Durban 400 mile race in a 3.8, despite driving with a shattered windscreen.

By 1964 the Jauar Mark II domination was severely threatened not by the big American giants but by the formidable Lotus Cortinas. Nevertheless there were still a few aces in the pack; in the 1964 Tour de France Bernard Consten made the best aggregate performance in the hillclimb and came a creditable third, although Texier with Marie Louise Mermod this time won the ladies award in the touring car category. In the E.T.C. round at Zandvoort John Sparrow won his class in 1628 VC, also taking second in class at Nuremberg.

Marks IIs returning to the racetracks. The white car is a genuine Coombs-modified example.

Mark IIs in the paddock at a JDC Inter-Area Challenge meeting.

The Mark II 3.8 prepared for the 1960 New York Motor Show,
complete with gold-plated trim and period gold-plated model.

A JDC member receives a trophy.

The exciting 340/380 model. The car depicted is the only known survivor of the handful made.

Brands Hatch circuit again, and two historic Mark IIs still competing in 1968.

Further, at Zolder he took second place behind the Nocker 3.8 and at Zandvoort he excelled by taking first place. Throughout 1964 and into 1966 Jaguar still kept their head above water with the Mark II, especially with Bob Jane in Australia, who marked up some considerable successes. In Europe John Sparrow and Peter Nocker were still competing in their old cars, John making second place at Spa and Peter fifth, and at Goodwood in April B.E. Rutland competed in an old 3.8. Many other Mark IIs participated in Club events, but through the late sixties and early seventies fewer and fewer Mark IIs were to be seen in competition and Jaguar's competitive efforts in general were at a very low ebb. As had been the fate of the Mark Is, many Mark IIs were relegated to the realms of banger racing, etc.

With the growth of interest in classic cars and in particular vehicles of the late fifties and early sixties, enthusiasm for competitive sport flourished. One-make car clubs expanded their activities dramatically. On the competitive front the pre '57 Classic Saloon Car Championship was born, and once again

Some of the JDC Inter-Area Challenge team preparing at Silverstone for another race.

the cars took to the circuits. This championship, although very successful, did little to encourage the compact Jaguars back to the tracks as only the very early Mark Is were eligible.

An enthusiastic member of the Jaguar Drivers' Club, Jim Lowry, therefore drew up a set of rules to enable saloons from the mid sixties to compete in a championship all of their own. The first set of regulations were fairly lax and were designed to cover the sort of modifications that might be expected of cars in the 1980s. This meant that at the time it was possible to compete in a Mark II with a triple-carburettor E Type engine!

The first three events were arranged for 1982, commencing with the first round at Silverstone. The race proved an overwhelming success, popular with the promoters, competitors and spectators – indeed the race boasted a near complete grid of cars. Not for twenty years had so many Jaguars competed together. The event received national publicity and enthusiasm grew – the Jaguar Drivers' Club Inter-Area Challenge Series was born.

For 1983 the Challenge was expanded into an eight race series;

Even today the Mark IIs look right on the track. Here two enthusiastic owners compete at Silverstone in a club event.

competitors used the winter months to prepare their cars and improved vehicles with more experienced drivers fought for the title that year. For 1984 the regulations were changed again, limiting modifications and containing costs. Mark Is and Mark IIs are restricted to two carburettors of a maximum 2″ diameter. Firmer suspension and a modified braking system are allowed and most competitors now run on XJ6 wheels and tyres for extra grip. All such modifications are relatively inexpensive and such a combination produces close racing where money plays little part, but individual ability is paramount.

Most of the cars are also used as everyday transport and in some cases even pull the family caravan at holiday time! There is a tremendous feeling of comradeship between all competitors which will ensure the future success of the series. The Mark Is and IIs have returned to fight again.

Mark I leads Mark II in very murky conditions.

Purchase, Maintenance and Restoration

Let us now look at purchase. First the prospective buyer must decide on the model which most interests him – or perhaps price may be the governing factor. The range of models covered in this book is extensive enough to ensure that any enthusiast of the marque can find a model to match his individual requirements, and for this purpose the range can be split up into three main groups, the Mark Is, Mark IIs (including the later 240 and 340 models) and Daimlers.

The earlier Mark I cars have a distinctive charm and character all of their own. They were, after all, the first of a long line of very successful Jaguars and their basic engineering was right first time. As discussed earlier the Mark Is were marginally quicker than their Mark II counterparts and, some might argue, more solidly built. They were certainly of more period appearance. Mark Is were also undeniably comfortable, with bucket type front seats giving superb lateral support more in keeping with the sporting saloon image.

The survival rate of Mark Is has been considerably worse than that of the later cars. Upon the release of the Mark IIs in 1959 the Mark Is instantly became the lost sheep of the family and were soon cast off by their owners in favour of the new models. Secondhand prices dropped sharply and even buyers in the lower price range preferred to wait until they could afford a cheap Mark II. A lot of Mark Is went to the scrapyard when their resale value had dropped significantly as they were not cheap to maintain and, of course, no-one at that time considered restoration a viable proposition.

On scarcity value alone, then, the Mark Is should have proved highly collectable, but over the last few years the Mark IIs have continued to outshine the earlier cars. Although the earlier cars are rare, prices still have not risen accordingly, and a good example can be purchased at a much lower price than a comparable Mark II. If one is looking for a very practical and attractive car that is both rare and unusual, then a Mark I is a very good buy and will prove excellent value for money.

As to which Mark I model to buy, the later 3.4 litre cars with disc brakes are usually considered to be the most desirable. They were certainly the quickest, and with disc brakes are still decidedly more practical than many other classic cars. 3.4s are also the rarest of the breed, this scarcity highlighted by the very small number of 3.4s registered with the Jaguar clubs. The early 2.4s should not be overlooked. With the cast radiator grille and full spats covering the rear wheels, they were very attractive as well as having the honour of being the first of the line. The Achilles heel of the early 2.4 was the drum brakes, which are decidedly inferior.

As most of the mechanical items on the Mark I were the same as on the later models spares availability is reasonably good. Although it is unlikely that you will find a Mark I in a scrapyard these days, most Mark II parts can be made to fit. Body panels, however, where they differ from the Mark II, are a significant problem. There are now very few original Mark I panels around, and where such items do exist prices will inevitably be high. No-one as yet has started to re-make Mark I panels, and because of the small number of cars still in existence, it is unlikely that anyone will start. Mark II front wings can be modified and adapted to fit a Mark I, as can the bottom sections of the doors. Chromium and other exterior trim items present no real problems – even the early cast radiator grilles seem to be in plentiful supply. Some specialist items can give a little trouble, like the script from the boot lid.

Interior trim is an expensive aspect and must be considered when contemplating the purchase or restoration of a Mark I. As all the seating is leather, a full retrim is very expensive. Here again there is only a slim chance of finding a set of upholstery from another car in good condition, so beware the car with severely damaged or non-existent upholstery. Door trims (not leather) and carpets should not create a major problem and woodwork can easily be renovated provided nothing of importance is missing.

It pays then to seek out a Mark I in reasonable condition (more so than with any other model within the scope of this book) and avoid non-runners that require total restoration. It is my advice therefore to seek out the best one can afford, if necessary disregarding personal preferences for a 2.4, 3.4, manual, automatic, etc.

If your choice is a Mark II, then the range of options is much wider, with the three engine sizes plus the later 240/340 models. As with the Mark I, early cars, with some of their unusual features, could be considered a little more collectable, but few of these pre-'61 cars still survive in anything like restorable condition. In contrast the very last of the range, the 240 and 340, have long been shunned by the majority of enthusiasts, who have considered them to be cheap and nasty with 'plastic' upholstery and odd looking bumpers. To be fair these cars were quicker than the earlier Mark IIs and the 240 was a particularly popular version. 340s are very rare as only 2800 were manufactured (left and right hand drive) and therefore they must be desirable. As for the Ambla upholstery, in some ways this can be an advantage: most Ambla upholstered cars stood the test of time and can still look like new, and with the high cost of replacing leather trim Ambla must surely be worth considering.

The full-bodied Mark IIs with thick bumpers and leather upholstery are still considered to be the most collectable, and of the three engine sizes the 3.8 version is the one to go for. The ultimate Mark II must be a 3.8 litre with manual/overdrive transmission (preferably the later all-synchromesh version), wire wheels and power assisted steering. Models with this specification fetch the most money and hold their prices well. Next in line is the 3.4 litre car, again the manual version with the same options. The 3.4 litre is generally considered to be the smoothest of the three engines, slightly cheaper to insure than the 3.8 although not much (if any) cheaper to run. More 3.4s were produced than any other model and this popularity continues today. The 2.4 litre cars do not have a great deal of 'sparkle' and are not as fast or economical as the earlier Mark Is or later 240s.

Automatic transmission versions are particularly disappointing to many as the engine is just not flexible enough to make up for the power loss through the gearbox. Because of the lack of popularity of the 2.4 litre cars, prices have been kept down and as such they are a good buy. 2.4s when new tended to be owned by the more sedate driver, and thus can in many instances be in better condition mechanically than the larger engined models. Bear in mind, however, that even the last cars were produced a long, long time ago and have probably passed through many owners' hands.

It is, of course, up to the individual to decide on the particular model which will most suit his or her circumstances and requirements. For instance, although I quote the 3.8 litre Mark II as the most desirable, I personally own a 3.4 version, which, after owning fourteen Mark IIs (including a 3.8) was a purchase I made from choice that I still stand by today. Mark IIs are still in reasonably plentiful supply and it would be wiser to purchase a low mileage, one owner 2.4 rather than a tatty 'ripe for restoration' 3.8 – no Jaguar is cheap to restore so buy the best your pocket can afford.

On to the Daimlers now, and these can offer a different style of motoring and appeal, complimenting rather than competing with the Jaguars. The most desirable of the models is the later V8 250, which provides the best of both worlds. These cars with the thinner bumpers were lighter and therefore slightly faster, yet maintained the luxury touches lacking in the Jaguar equivalents – leather upholstery, fog lamps and reclining seats. Manual transmission models are particularly rare and are therefore highly desirable. The earlier 2.5 V8 cars with the standard automatic transmission were a little

A typical long-term Mark I restoration project.

dull and lacked performance.

Daimlers made a very slow start in the classic car stakes and were generally considered less desirable than the equivalent Jaguar models. This situation has now changed dramatically, with Daimlers fetching much higher prices, although rarely as high as a top 3.8. Daimler owners tended to look after their cars better, and it is still not unusual to find a one or two owner example with a low mileage in quite outstanding condition. The particularly smooth V8 power unit is a major plus item in the car's favour.

As a general guide to the current popularity of the various models within the scope of this book, I recently carried out a survey based on the number of cars advertised for sale through various motoring journals over a period of six months, on the assumption that those cars not re-advertised were sold. The popularity listing is very approximate as the statistics can be varied according to different criteria. For example the number of cars advertised does not take into consideration the original production figures or the survival rate of each model. Nevertheless it is an interesting exercise for perusal:

(No. 1 was the most popular, No. 2 next, etc.)

No. 1	3.8 litre Mark II Manual
No. 2	3.4 litre Mark II Manual
No. 3	3.4 litre Mark II Automatic
No. 4	V8 250 (survey not large enough to differentiate between manual and automatic versions)
No. 5	240 Manual
No. 6	2.4 litre Mark II Manual
No. 7	2.5 V8
No. 8	2.4 litre Mark II Automatic
No. 9	240 Automatic
No. 10	3.8 litre Mark II Automatic
No. 11	2.4 litre Mark I ⎫
No. 12	340 ⎬ (survey not large enough to differentiate between manual and automatic versions)
No. 13	3.4 litre Mark I ⎭

It is interesting to consider that the 3.4 litre Mark I is *apparently* the least popular. Would it have been more popular now if more had been produced?

Assuming that the prospective buyer has decided on a particular model let us now look at the pleasures and pitfalls of actually making the purchase. Whilst many people have made a snap decision after viewing gleaming paintwork and shining chrome and after listening to the smooth sales patter of the vendor emphasising the benefits of his car, these days it its imperative to pay more attention to detail before finalising the purchase. Restoration is getting dearer and dearer as the work is necessarily labour intensive. As the majority of enthusiasts do not have bottomless pockets to finance such expense it is vital to look very critically at any intended purchase.

The single most important aspect to investigate is the bodywork. Jaguars of this period were no different from any other mass-produced car in that they were built to a price, with little consideration to water traps or adequate rustproofing. Many cars offered for sale today are therefore suffering badly from 'rust bug' and many apparently nice looking models are not at all what they seem. Filler, old oil cans and even cardboard are used to disguise major deterioration of the bodywork. Replacement body panels can prove to be very expensive and as all the cars covered in this book are of the monocoque form of construction, the strength of the whole car lies in certain key areas. If these areas are badly corroded, then the car must be considered totally unroadworthy.

As far as the general exterior appearance is concerned, whilst it would be nice to go prodding with a good screwdriver and hefty hammer, this is not practical, so the points to watch for at a glance are ill-fitting panels. The gaps between doors and other panels should all be relatively even, and look for ripples or unevenness in the shaping of the bodywork. Give particular attention to newly painted areas and freshly undersealed sections.

Taking a more serious and detailed look at the exterior bodywork, let us start at the front, bearing in mind that the points mentioned relate to all models unless specifically stated. The front valance which runs across the full width of the car just behind the bumper is prone to rusting, particularly in the centre where it dips and curves to match the shape of the radiator grille. Underneath the valance is a crossmember which collects dirt and grime from the road wheels, and this rusts through very easily. Neither of these sections should be of great concern, especially the crossmember, which is readily replaceable at a low cost if not repairable. At either end of the crossmember leading to the extreme front curvature inside the front wings there are small panels known as crow's feet (because of their shaping). These support the leading edges of the wings and again are very prone to rust. As with the crossmember however, they are easily replaceable with re-manufactured panels at reasonable cost.

A Mark II that looked good when purchased a few weeks earlier. After some rubbing down major rot and filler soon appeared.

Front end showing the vulnerable 'crows feet' and crossmember, common rust areas.

The front wings themselves rust in many places and are extremely expensive to replace, although fortunately various sections are now available separately to relieve body rot in isolated areas. The sidelight housings on Mark IIs and Daimlers are particularly vulnerable to the collection of water, the first signs of trouble here being bubbles in the surrounding paintwork, and the weld marks (where the housings join the wings) showing through the paint. Rust is also a problem around the indicator lights (sidelights on Mark Is) as mud collects behind the fittings on the inside of the wing, not usually detectable until the light fittings are removed. The extreme edges of the wheel arches also form a mud trap as water collects on the inside lip – again the first signs are paint bubbles. The rear half of the front wings does not escape trouble either. Water collects up around the edges of the inner closing panels. These panels are sealed to the wings by a rubber strip which deteriorates with age allowing the water to seep through. The result is rusting of the bottom of

Slight bubbling on this Mark II front wing when rubbed-down on the other wing revealed more severe problems.

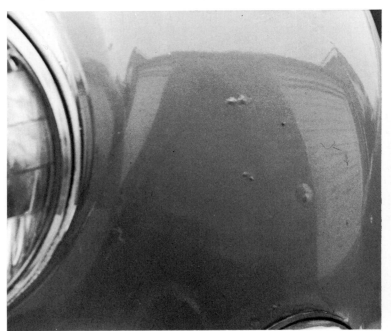

the front wing as well as damage to the sills. The closing panels are again easily replaceable, but do not fit them without inspecting the inner bodywork. At the very bottom edge of the front wings water settles in a trough around the curvature, gradually rotting away the whole section. As one can see, the front wings could prove one of the most expensive aspects of body repair.

The under-bonnet areas are relatively free from rust problems although the inner wings can rot away at the rear, especially near the bonnet hinges. The bonnet itself presents no problems. As the battery is located at the rear of the engine bay against the bulkhead, this could be an area of concern. Once the battery starts to leak, the acid will soon destroy the bulkhead behind, in many cases unnoticed until the battery is removed revealing major corrosion.

In the centre section of the bodywork the most important points are the floor pan and inner sills. The floor pan may well have started to rust through at the front, caused by water seepage from the wing area as mentioned above. Even more important are the inner sills, which cannot be seen from a general view of the car's exterior. Getting underneath the car and looking outwards towards the sills, the inner sills are the flat vertical sections of metal running along the insides of the sills. Rot here is structural and will require immediate surgery. The outer sills are not structural and previous owners may well have fitted cheap over-sills to make the car look attractive. This is a bad measure as underneath the over-sills rot is continuing to damage good metal, eventually

Inside the front wing, rust will attack the brake vacuum storage tank and its shield.

Still on the front wings, bubbles around the wheel-arch edge and at the bottom of the rear section of the wings usually indicate severe rusting.

The front wing on this car looked reasonable upon first inspection, but investigation revealed that a tin can had been fixed to the rotten wing and smoothed in with filler!

destroying the whole car. Proper sills are common enough to find and are cheap and relatively easy to replace. The four jacking points (two per side) on these cars are situated underneath the sills, adjacent to the wheels, and prove a common rust problem. Cleaned out regularly and suitably protected they should remain in good condition. New sections are available but are intricate to make and therefore expensive, and on some cars they have now been eliminated to save cost! The doors should open and close easily – on new cars the doors closed with a whisper (especially on Mark Is). The door bottoms are very prone to rust out as the window sealing was never that effective, allowing the passage of water down the inside of the door frame. If the drain holes were

Sidelight sections, wheel-arch sections and wing closing panels can now all be purchased to repair rust-damaged panels.

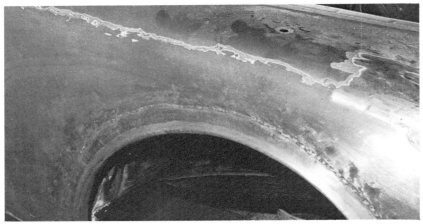

blocked up (a regular fault) the water remained trapped, eating its way through to the outer skin. Secondhand doors are still obtainable from a lot of sources although most will have some degree of deterioration in the same areas. The main frames of the doors are strong and rarely present any major rusting problems, so it is possible to re-skin the outer section, but this is not a job for the amateur. The door sealing rubbers will, with the passage of time, deteriorate to the point where they allow wind and water to enter the interior – or at worst will hold water, causing further rusting. Rubbers are now much easier to come by as similar section rubber is now available from several suppliers, but these seals do not come cheap.

Returning to the seat pan area, at the rear this time, this is a crucial area for inspection. When considering a suitable car, if it is at all possible to remove the rear seat this should reveal the offending areas for close examination. The specific areas are around the corners of the seat pan where the rear seat meets the floor, the edges of the upper section where they meet the wheel arches and all along the rear edge of the pan. Rusting of the rear wheel arches themselves can also be investigated much more easily with the rear seat removed. Inspect the whole rear end of the car very carefully as the axle, springs, etc., are all connected at this point. Looking inside the boot and removing the hardura matting will reveal any further rust problems. Any rot in the corners near the shock absorber mounting points denotes a serious case and the remainder of the car should therefore be stringently investigated. If it is practical to remove the hardboard panels on the sides of the boot, this will reveal the extent of any rusting around the boot floor edges, inside the wings (rarely a problem) and wheelarch sections. Underneath the boot floor, removing the spare wheel will probably reveal some degree of rust in the well, not crucial but it could be awkward to repair satisfactorily.

top left
The bottom edges of doors are a common cause of rusting through drain holes becoming blocked. Tell-tale signs are bubbles appearing.

top right
New wheel-arch repair sections for Mark I and II front wings, now readily and cheaply available.

bottom left
With the use of original factory tooling, complete new front wings can now be purchased.

bottom right
A new sill-section being installed on a Mark I.

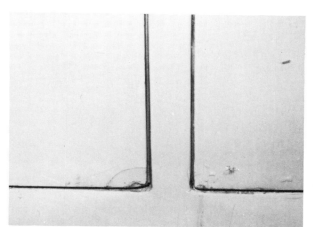

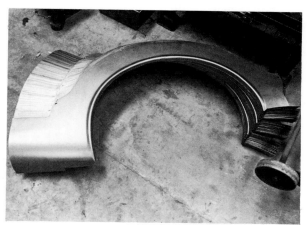

On the outside of the car again, look for rusting at the bottom of the rear wings, also at the lower edge of the boot lid itself. Rust here is caused because the sealing rubber deteriorates with age and collects water. The rear wheel spat covers are another common area for trouble. The earlier full spats are much more difficult and expensive to replace, now needing to be hand-made. The cut-away type rust quicker but supply is no longer a problem as newly manufactured items are available. Around the edge of the wheel arch itself the sealing strip may well have been neglected and will consequently hold water, leading to rust yet again. Finally the rear valance behind the back bumper bar can also give trouble as mud is forced up from the back wheels. Although the valance may look good from the outside, inspect the area from the inside, especially around the bumper mounting rubbers. As can be seen from the above there are few places on the Mark I or Mark II bodyshell that escape the dreaded rust-bug so I cannot emphasise too strongly the need to inspect this aspect of the car carefully.

As far as the mechanical aspects of these cars are concerned, they are strongly built, long-lived and generally trouble free. Provided the suspension, brakes and steering are regularly maintained, they should not give rise to any major problems. On the front suspension there are two grease nipples each side of the wishbone, and the inner ends of the top wishbones are adjustable for castor and camber angles. A loss of ride height and a drooping effect at the front end can amount to tired coil springs, which should be replaced to avoid grounding of the sump or exhaust pipes. The whole front subframe is mounted via Metalastic rubber blocks which after a time will deteriorate,

below
This shows just how rotten Mark I and II sills can get.

right
Typical rear-seat pan and wheel arch panel work necessary on these cars.

right
Removal of the rear seat can reveal horrible sights like this.

far right
Common rusting problem around the Panhard rod mounting.

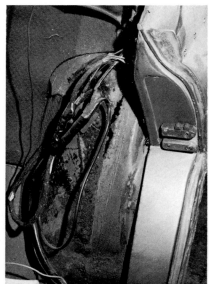

126

below
More severe rusting, this time taking away part of the swing mounting area.

right
Inside the boot now, and more rust in the wheel arches can be detected.

perish and split, in some cases shearing completely and causing a general sloppiness. These are easily replaceable and a must to ensure safety on the road. Steering on all cars is absolutely trouble free. It should be remembered that these cars are renowned for their low geared and heavy steering, so this should not give rise to worries about the system. Ball joints should be regularly attended to, the bottom joints being shimmed for adjustment, although adjustments will not be the same on both sides. Power steering, where fitted, is again generally reliable. If the unit is noisy and a little ineffective in use, then a fair amount of wear may have already taken place.

above
Slight bubbling around the bottom of the rear wing can lead to much more severe problems.

right
Rust in its most severe form can cause the petrol tank and spare wheel carrier literally to fall apart.

At the rear the springs are subject to a great amount of stress and inspecting the spring hangers is imperative. In many cases the box section holding the springs may have collapsed, allowing the springs to rest directly on the bodywork, sometimes without the knowledge of the owner, the only tell-tale being a slight droop at the rear often attributed to weak springs. The Panhard rod connection is also an important aspect and has always been a common failure on these cars, in many cases breaking from its mounting within a few months of production. This is by no means a major problem as the mounting can be easily welded back into place with the offside rear wheel removed. The rear springs themselves tend to settle, giving the effect of a drooping rear end. When they reach this stage, they should be replaced as insufficient clearance between the tyres and wheel arches will result. It is also not uncommon for the top leaves of the springs to break, giving the car a lop-sided look when on level ground.

Back axles hardly ever give trouble although the limited slip units can become excessively noisy if the correct oil additive has not been used. In some cases axles may have been changed and if the ratios were not the same a drop in performance or fuel consumption could result, or at the very least incorrect speedometer readings. The torsion bars connecting the axle to the body have rubber bush inserts which deteriorate in time causing knocking sounds on bumps, under acceleration or braking. These should be inspected regularly.

The drum braked cars are trouble free but the early disc brakes as fitted to the original 2.4 and 3.4 are a little awkward as the wheel cylinders have to be dismantled to change the pads. The later systems are much easier to maintain and if regularly inspected and looked after will give little trouble. If neglected, spares can be very expensive. The most common problems are rusty discs, seized wheel cylinders and, if the pedal pressure is rather heavy, problems with the servo. A general sluggishness in the hydraulic brake system is usually attributable to old fluid absorbing water, which could cause damage to the seals and brake pipes. Another common brake problem concerns the vacuum storage tank positioned underneath the offside front wing. The tank, shield and valve are all in direct contact with dirt thrown up by the front offside wheel and rusting easily takes place without constant attention. Once the tank is penetrated by rust the engine only generates enough vacuum to allow the servo to operate when the car is running, allowing no backup when the engine is switched off. Again, parts are easily available and not difficult to fit. Jaguars have a reputation for ineffective handbrakes. Adjusted correctly there is no reson why an efficient brake cannot be obtained. The problems are usually caused by a seized fulcrum bolt adjacent to the rear brake caliper or the improper adjustment of the cables.

Jaguar gearboxes are immensely strong units and the only problems likely to be encountered would involve the earlier Moss gearbox (without synchromesh on first gear). Replacements for these boxes are difficult to come by, especially the layshaft. Although the box is normally quite noisy in first and reverse gears, beware of excessive noise, which is a clear sign of trouble. Overdrive units where fitted should be reliable and should operate cleanly without undue delay, the major problem associated with the units being the electrical solenoid sticking and dirt accumulating fetched in from the gearbox. Clean the filters regularly and there should be little trouble. If trouble does exist and the car sticks in overdrive, never attempt to reverse the car; this will cause severe damage to the unit. Automatic transmissions are also generally reliable, usually only requiring basic adjustment, although the early DG units fitted to some Mark IIs can present some spares difficulty and are notorious for oil leaks.

Clutches on Jaguars have quite a long life if treated with respect but it should be noted that the engine has to be removed for clutch replacement, which should be considered if buying a car with a slipping clutch. In some extreme cases previous owners may well have 'hacked out' part of the floor pan to enable the clutch to be replaced without removing the engine. Look for such vandalism and avoid these cars like the plague, as it is more than likely that other short-cuts will have been taken to keep the car on the road.

Jaguar engines are particularly well engineered and strong and should prove good for at least 100,000 miles without any major overhaul if maintained correctly. However, do not think that a cheap car which is good in the body but has a bad engine is a good buy – engine rebuilds are very expensive, costing well into four figures.

The XK engines are prone to oil leaks and it is very rare to find an engine totally leak free. Watch out, however, for severe leaks from the rear of the engine, most probably caused by the rear main oil seal, replacing which requires the engine to be removed from the body. In fact any work that requires engine removal can be troublesome as the units are very heavy, cumbersome and awkward to manoeuvre around the tight engine bay of these cars. Even where engine removal is not necessary, in certain other cases like sump removal, the front subframe must be taken down, again time consuming and costly if not done by oneself.

The engine should be reasonably quiet although a certain amount of tappet noise is to be expected and is not unhealthy. Oil pressure should be a minimum of 40psi at 3,000rpm and should not drop below 15/20psi on tick-over, although pressure at the upper rev. range is more important. Look for smoke emitted from the exhaust on the over-run, normally caused by the valve guides wearing, although a faint blue haze is normal, especially with the 3.8 litre engines, which normally burn a little oil. Revving the engine to between 1,500 and 2,000rpm will show up any timing chain rattle, another common fault on the XK engines which can prove expensive. The upper timing chain (recognisable from the source of the noise) is adjustable without much trouble but the bottom chain necessitates the removal of the engine. All Jaguar engines are renowned for their thirst for oil so this should not be a cause for concern. The cylinder heads, being of aluminium, are prone to corrosion unless proper anti-freeze levels are maintained throughout the year.

Referring now to the Daimler V8 engines, these are also generally very reliable. Renowned for their silence and smoothness, these units should never be noisy. Oil pressure should read between 35 and 40psi at normal running speeds and at least 15psi at tickover. Piston wear was a problem on early engines and in some cases the entire crown could detach itself from the piston body. The pistons were modified on engines produced after 1967. The exhaust valves can stay open due to carbon build up and the aluminium heads can corrode as with the Jaguar units. After 30-50,000 miles the centre three of the five crankshaft bearings are likely to have narrowed and to need replacement, although this job can be done with the engine in situ. As the distributor has two sets of points, it is important that they receive regular attention to ensure efficient running. Oil consumption on the V8 engines is as bad as if not worse than on the Jaguar units and figures have been recorded as low as 150mpp even on good engines.

The fuel system on all cars should give little trouble. The simple S.U. fuel pump is easily and cheaply replaceable but the fuel tank itself, which is situated underneath the boot adjacent to the spare wheel well, is in a very vulnerable position and is therefore subject to the ravages of salt and rain. It is quite common for the tank to rot away at the top front and underneath near the drain plug. These tanks can be replaced but are relatively expensive. Alternatively repairs can be carried out if not too badly rotted.

Exterior trim is getting harder to find. In most cases Mazak cast metal was used and this is not suitable for rechroming. Door handles were common to many other Jaguar saloons and therefore should not prove too difficult to replace. Chrome beading is now getting particularly difficult to find either new or in good secondhand condition. Light units are not too difficult to find as there are still plenty of new ones about, although expensive in some cases. Mark I front side lights and rear lights are now being made. The front units are not common to any other model and the same applies to the rear ones (these often get taken for Mark VII units but are slightly different).

As far as the interior is concerned, carpets are quite inexpensive to replace and are readily available from a number of sources, but beware the type of carpet material, which varied several times during manufacture, if originality is your aim. Woodwork can be revarnished, bringing it back to an as new condition. Greater attention should be paid to the seating, especially if trimmed in leather. Leather is an expensive commodity and to have new hides made up is very costly. To retrim a Mark II would take about five hides and would easily cost into four figures. Several firms are now offering ready-made leather seat covers for the Mark II in a variety of original colour schemes, but the cost is still high. Alternatively, mildly scuffed and scratched leather can be rejuvenated by renovation kits available by mail order from Connolly Bros and other reputable firms. The effects of rejuvenating leather can be quite striking. Mark I and the later Daimler V8 250 seats can cause more of a problem. Ready-made covers are not available for these models, meaning that a one-off order needs to be placed with the upholsterer. The problem with the Daimlers is the ventilated panels, which not every upholstery firm can reproduce.

The door trims and other ancillary trim items like the centre console of the Mark IIs were all made in vinyl to simulate leather and keep costs down. This material is cheap enough to buy and easy enough to work with. The door panels may create a problem if originality is to be maintained as on most

Door trim panels may only look slightly wrinkled at first but their removal shows how water can get trapped, rotting away the board backing.

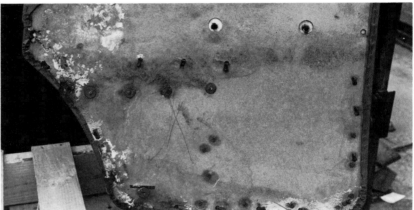

models heat seams were moulded into the panels for effect. Fortunately, at least one firm now reproduces the panels complete with back-boards to original specification and at quite reasonable cost.

The other item worth investigating in the interior is the headlining. This is quite easy to replace on the Mark Is and later Mark IIs but the early Mark IIs (with inset sun-visors) and Daimlers are a little more difficult. The main areas of concern are tears and dampness, the latter caused by water seeping in through the rear window, a very common occurrence on Jaguars. If the headlining is generally in good condition but dirty, it can be cleaned in situ but care should be taken not to wet the surface too much as this causes wrinkles when dry.

Normal everyday maintenance on any of the models should not prove any more expensive or troublesome than with other classic cars. In many respects parts will be cheaper due to the ready availability of items and the interchangeability of components with other Jaguars.

In this book it has only been possible to touch on the many aspects of maintenance and restoration of these cars. For much more detailed information and advice on the models concerned, it is strongly recommended that anyone interested should join one of the clubs. The Jaguar Drivers' Club has a very active Register specifically dealing with the Mark Is, IIs and 240/340s and covering all aspects including competition. The Jaguar Enthusiasts' Club has a strong interest in the practical aspects of Jaguar ownership. It has a parts department, a parts location service and technical advisers, and remanufactures special tools. For Daimlers there is the Daimler and Lanchester Owners' Club Limited, which has a special Register looking after the 2.5 and V8 250 models and can supply a wide range of parts for them. Further details of these and overseas clubs may be found at the back of this book.

Mark I and II Miscellany

From the introduction of the first Mark I to the last 240, numerous cars were modified either for racing, rallying, specialist purposes or just for fun. Some of these cars still exist, others have passed into oblivion but all had their attributes and we will discuss a few of them here. On another theme, the toy and model manufacturers have always looked kindly on the compact Jaguars and we will also discuss some of the better known examples.

When Jaguars initially launched the 2.4 in 1956 it did not take one toy manufacturer (Corgi) long to produce a well detailed die-cast version in their ⅟₄₃rd scale. The model was well proportioned but took the form of a fire brigade vehicle – I doubt the authenticity here! Between 1957 and 1958 the model was available in several variants: the fire car, standard saloon and saloon with working suspension and plastic windows. A particularly rare model is the Corgi saloon with friction drive. Also in 1957 the Mettoy company issued a ⅟₁₆th scale plastic and metal motorised toy in very small numbers but particularly good in detail. This model was battery driven. Also in that year Roco-Peetzy, an Austrian firm, produced a plastic 2.4. In the late fifties Mak's produced a range of Mark I 2.4s approximately 6″ long in plastic made up either as a saloon, police car or fire chief's car for limited distribution. The well known Lincoln International toy company also produced a range of 2.4s in various colours to ⅟₂₀th, ⅟₃₂nd and ⅟₄₃rd scales, all in plastic and in varying colours, friction drive, battery, battery remote controlled or free running.

In 1959 the Lesney company produced a matchbox 3.4 litre Mark I to ⅟₇₂nd scale with plastic or metal wheels and in the same year the British company Startex produced a ⅟₃₂nd tinplate 2.4 motorised by pulling out the exhaust pipe! At the end of 1960 (after production of the Mark I had finished) Tri-ang under the Spot-On name issued a 3.4 litre Mark I, die-cast to ⅟₄₂nd scale in powder blue or white, and later as a police car in white or black. Later still, in 1963, T.A.T. of Hong Kong produced a ⅟₄₃rd scale plastic friction driven 2.4 for a short while and last of all Kelloggs issued a free plastic Mark I toy (of unknown origin) in every cereal packet for a limited period.

Friction driven 2.4 Fire Car from the fifties.

Since this time many of the above 'toys' have become collectors' models. Grand Prix models and the Mik-an-Sue model company are now producing 'new' Mark I models either as kits or in ready assembled and painted form. Digressing from die-casts and plastics for a moment, the Tri-ang company once produced a miniature slot-racing set known as Minic roadways and amongst the model cars available were two Mark Is, one in red, the other in cream with racing stripes.

As with the real thing, Mark IIs have to some extent been better catered for on the toy and model scene. Meccano were the first to introduce a model, in their Dinky Toys range, to ¼₃rd scale in 1960. The toy was a die-cast 3.4 Mark II available in a variety of colours including maroon, grey or cream, with plastic windows, suspension and steering. Later the model was supplemented (in 1962) by a white police car version, complete with blue light and aerial. Also in 1962 Matchbox upgraded their old Mark I mould, turning it into a 3.4 Mark II with opening bonnet revealing a detailed engine bay. In 1961 Revell of the U.S.A. produced a plastic kit based on the 3.4. In 1963 Norev of France produced a plastic ¼₃rd scale 2.4 Mark II, although with little detail. At the same time the Hong Kong company of Bandai produced a ½₄th scale tinplate friction driven 3.4, changing the design to a police car one year later. Minic updated their Mark Is to 3.4 Mark IIs in 1965 as a standard saloon, rally saloon or police motorway patrol car.

To date the only known Mark II model being specially produced is the Grand Prix version in two forms, the 'home market' model in silver with disc wheels and the 'export' model in red with wire wheels and left hand drive. The only Daimler model I have ever been able to find was of Dinky origin produced from the Mark II Jaguar casting with a revised radiator grille.

Let us return now to the world of the full-size cars. In the late fifties many of the competitive drivers who raced and rallied Mark Is also used similar cars for everyday transport – after all, what else could they have driven? Graham Hill, Duncan Hamilton and Colin Chapman all ran Mark I 3.4s at some time and perhaps one of the most well known was Mike Hawthorn, who had a Mark I specially prepared by the factory to near racing standard. This 3.4, finished in British Racing Green, registered VDU 881, had an engine fitted with 9 to 1 pistons, two 2″ S.U. carburettors, a competition clutch and a specially made-up straight-through twin exhaust. Wide wheels were fitted to the rear giving an extra 2″ of track and the rear spats were suitably modified. Stiffened front springs were used and for the rear an extra leaf was added. Competition shock absorbers were fitted all round and the rear axle ratio was altered to 4.05 to 1 (from 3.77) giving the car tremendous acceleration, especially in second gear.

One of the ex-Betts Mark Is.

The 3.4 could reputably do about 130mph although I imagine it would have been rather unstable at such speeds. To allow for the speed of the car a 140mph speedometer was fitted. Marchal headlamps were used along with Raydyot fog and spot lights.

Mike Hawthorn sadly came to grief with the car as related earlier in this book, so it no longer exists. A replica of his car does exist. Modified by Jaguar to Hawthorn's specification, it was purchased shortly after his death by a Mr Ditcham but has now passed through at least two other owners. The car is registered 220 LPE and is finished in British Racing Green with matching wire wheels just as the Hawthorn car. To date the car has covered a nominal mileage and is being preserved in its original condition.

Another of the famous Mark Is, the 3.4 modified by John Coombs and raced by Roy Salvadori, then taken over by Peter Sargeant, is reputedly still around in the London area although no further details are known. This was one of the ultimate Mark Is, heavily modified with 10 to 1 compression pistons, oversize valves, twin 2″ S.U. carburettors, larger (XK120) sump, competition clutch, close ratio gearbox (still with overdrive), Power-Lok limited slip differential, stiffened suspension with modified camber and a widened rear track. Bucket seats were fitted for the driver and front seat passenger and alloy doors, bootlid and bonnet were fitted for lightness (although the driver's door was in steel for strength). There was some rumour that the car was later fitted with three 2″ S.U. carburettors but this is unsubstantiated.

Deeper into the racing scene and the ex-Alfie Betts 'Green Bean' Mark I, registered UXF 363, is still around today. This was extensively modified with glass-fibre panels for lightness and a 3.8 litre engine. The car was apparently sold quite recently but still retains most of its modifications. Many modified

cars have hit the headlines again on the current racing scene, like the 2.4 Mark I of Andrew Moore-Hinton and the 2.4 of Roger Andreason (7KMD). John Young, strong supporter of the Mark I/II Inter-Area Challenge, has recently acquired the ex-Frank Brown rally Mark I FWB 1, now re-registered. After leaving Frank Brown's hands this car passed to his co-driver and was rallied further. From then it passed through only one other owner until John bought the car, still complete with all original documentation, rally sheets, etc. The car has been standing for some considerable time and therefore is being extensively restored at John's own garage, J.Y. Sports Cars, hopefully to race again in the not too distant future. This is the only rally Mark I known to survive.

Only one of the original Jaguar Cars demonstrators is known to have survived, this being PVC 302, a black 2.4 recently advertised for sale in apparently concours condition.

Last but not least on the Mark I scene were the special purpose vehicles – no, not the Fire Service car as depicted by Corgi toys but something very similar, police patrol cars. For years Jaguars have been used by various constabularies. In the thirties and forties SS saloons and Mark Vs were extensively used by the police, especially in the rural areas. Mark VIIs were used in Scotland and for CID cars in London during the early fifties but the most popular Jaguar for police duties at this time was the 2.4 litre Mark I. This model was extensively used in approximately twenty police authorities up and down the country. The model provided adequate power for most purposes and proved popular with the drivers. They found the cars comfortable and agile, particularly suited to the varied tasks of the mobile force.

Nearly all cars were supplied in black with tan interior and were virtually standard production cars with the exception of such items as loud-hailer, the chromium bell (usually attached to the front bumper), re-calibrated speedometer, radio telephone, twin rear view mirrors and POLICE signs situated either on the front and rear bumpers, on the roof or in the windows. Other cars were supplied 'unmarked' depending on duty requirements. The Jaguar Mark Is apparently lasted well in service, finally ousted by Mark IIs or Ford Zephyrs! Very few 3.4s were supplied to the police. As there were no motorways at this time, perhaps the authorities felt there was no need for the extra power of the 3.4 litre engine.

With regard to other uses for Mark Is, the situation is a little vague. Many cars, of course, were converted to a similar specification to that of the Mark II, with revised radiator grille, lights, engines, etc. In one case a car was converted to a pick-up although nothing is known of this vehicle. Mark Is were not of the size or stature to be used as limousines but in at least one case (South Africa) a 2.4 was used as official transport for a government official.

These two pictures are reproduced from a Jaguar promotional leaflet aimed at county constabularies.

One other interesting Mark I still to survive today is the 3.4 litre car at the Jaguar factory in Coventry. This black with red interior model was first registered in 1958 as a left-hand drive example with automatic transmission. The car belonged to Paul Frère, the famous racing driver and journalist, who has now loaned it to Jaguar on a semi-permanent basis.

Before leaving the Mark I, it is perhaps appropriate to mention the Coombs modified cars, of which the first was a 3.4 litre Mark I. Coombs and Son (Guildford) were well respected distributors of Jaguar cars for the Surrey area, who got involved in racing Mark Is in the late fifties. As you will already have read earlier in this book, the Coombs organisation employed the services of top rate drivers like Roy Salvadori, Graham Hill and others, making up a formidable racing team.

Unusual Mark I pick-up.

John Coombs displaying his modified 3.8 BUY 1. Note the special rear wheel arch treatment, vinyl roof and unlouvred bonnet.

As well as preparing their own cars for competition, Coombs also prepared cars to varying degrees of specification for private customers, which leads us to the first modified car, a 3.4 litre (registered 3309 NO) for a Mr Dunster in November/December 1958. The car regularly competed in various events in the late fifties and early sixties, driven by the owner. The last Coombs modified cars were produced around 1967 based on the 3.8 litre Mark II. In that period of nine years only about forty cars in total were modified and ever since there has been much speculation and myth surrounding the Coombs cars. There are a lot of cars around said to be of Coombs origin, and in extreme cases cars have actually been rebuilt with modifications to resemble the 'real thing' and add value.

Recently a lot of detailed information came to hand about the Coombs car from Mr Ken Bell (ex-employee of Coombs and now an official of the Jaguar Enthusiasts' Club) and I am indebted to him for help in preparing these pages and for the supply of many period photographs.

Below is the total list of known Coombs conversions including their own competition cars.

Model	Colour	Owner	Reg. No.	Comments
MkI 3.4	Black	Mr Dunster	3309 NO	Red interior, used for competition.
MkI 3.4	Pearl Grey	Coombs Ltd.	287 JPK	Official Coombs Race Car.
MkI 3.4	Maroon	Coombs Ltd.	TWK 287	Official Coombs Race Car.
MkII 3.8	Pearl Grey	Tim Powell	TP 28	New car with wide wheels, later written off, rebodied in Sherwood Green.
MkII 3.8	Old English White	Tony Dale	TD 2	New car.
MkII 3.8	Met. Grey	Dudley Weir	?	New car.

MkII 3.8	Met. Dark Blue	Bob Jennings	37 PF	Secondhand car. Wide wheels.
MkII 3.8	Pearl Grey	Tony Hubbard	?	Burnt out in Switzerland.
MkII 3.8	B.R.G.	British Jig & Crane Co.	?	Supplied new.
MkII 3.4	Pearl Grey	P. Woodroffe	4576 NK	Secondhand car for competition use. Later converted to 3.8 litre engine.
MkII 3.8	B.R.G.	Mr Jacobs	?	Supplied new.
MkII 3.8	Green or Blue	Mr Lakeland	?	Supplied new.
MkII 3.8	Met. Dark Blue	CF Anderson	?	Supplied new and extensively modified.
MkII 3.8	Met. Blue	PA Smith	JPA 432C	Supplied new.
MkII 3.8	B.R.G.	Mr Edwards	OVV 397	?
MkII 3.8	Sherwood Green	Mr Pepper	4 PPK	Supplied new.
MkII 3.8	Blue	Mr Pope	?	Supplied new.
MkII 3.8	Blue	Mr Foot	?	?
MkII 3.8	Cotswold Blue	Coombs Ltd	7 YPG	Coombs demonstrator.
MkII 3.8	Roman Mauve	N Streeter	?	Supplied new.
MkII 3.4	B.R.G.	D Ritchie	?	Personal car of Coombs employee.
MkII 3.8	Met. Blue	R Grimmond	?	Personal car of Coombs employee.
MkII 3.4	Old English White	H Bazely	34 DVD	Personal car of Coombs employee later converted to 3.8 litre and re-painted Pearl Grey.
MkII 3.4	Black	Mr Chalmers	?	?
MkII 3.8	Old English White	Mr K Bell	312 PE	Personal car of Coombs employee.
MkII 3.8	Pearl Grey	Coombs Ltd	8 TPL	Official Coombs Race Car.

The louvred bonnet rarely fitted to Coombs-modified cars.

As well as the above there were three or four 3.8 litre Mark IIs raced by Coombs under the registration numbers BUY 1 and BUY 12, all in Pearl Grey (Coombs racing colour) plus a further 3.4 litre model (details unknown) and a couple of other private 3.8s (one in red, one in beige or pearl grey, again details unknown). Coombs also modified an S Type 3.8 in the mid-sixties for a Mr Jacob who had previously run a Mark II Coombs car, and a little later a 4.2 litre E Type was also modified for a Mr Cazabon, finished in metallic dark green.

As you can see only three Mark Is in total were modified, two of which were for Coombs' own use in racing. There was a long gap before the first Mark II was converted, a 3.8 litre car in 1960. Mark IIs were in great demand when first released, and when eventually Coombs received a Mark II, it created a lot of attention from customers and employees alike. From that time on modified cars trickled through the Coombs workshop. They were in the main 3.8s with the odd 3.4, but conversions were never carried out on 2.4 litre cars. Most of the cars 'treated' were supplied new from the Jaguar factory, a few were secondhand and at least two cars (probably Coombs' own racing examples) were built up from bare bodyshells.

Outside racing circles, the Coombs organisation was best known in the Surrey and London area, so it is understandable that most of the cars modified went to buyers from these areas, and most of the cars returned to the Coombs workshops for regular maintenance and service. The modified cars never received a great deal of publicity, in fact it is fair to say that no-one at the company ever realised the commercial potential of promoting the modifications to the general Jaguar buying public, except, that is, for a period in 1963 when a brochure was printed listing all the modifications, with prices, and a fully modified car (7 YPG) was assembled as a demonstrator. I have only found reference to the car in two motoring publications from the period. First, *Autosport* of 1st June 1963 anounced the "newly introduced grand touring version of the 3.8 Mark II Jaguar marketed by Coombs and Sons (Guildford)." The mention was brief, with basic information about modifications and comparative speeds against an E Type.

The other magazine reference was in *Sporting Motorist* of August 1963, who actually borrowed 7 YPG for a roadtest. The article, entitled "A 'GT'-ed Jag from Coombs", included several photographs of the car and some details of the modifications from the Coombs brochure. The writer obviously liked the Coombs car, as he commented, "A few days with the Coombs modified 3.8

The Le Mans type petrol filler fitted to Coombs cars equipped with the auxiliary fuel tank.

Jaguar has proved to us that the lessons learned in many years of competing with these cars can be transferred to a road vehicle with highly satisfying, not to say sensational results." The writer went on, "It will outperform virtually any other make of car on the road. Even the 3.8's own sporting sister the E Type has very little on it in terms of acceleration, even though its maximum speed is rather higher. A clean pair of heels can be shown to other sporting cars costing upwards of £1,000 more." The car was found to be exceptionally smooth, yet taut and with a well-balanced feel, and none of the comfort or control of the vehicle had been lost. The suspension was found to be a little hard on some types of road surface and the car could prove noisy at high revs. Another unfortunate point concerned the fuel consumption, which dropped to around 14/15mpg even when driven reasonably carefully. These minor drawbacks did not reduce the writer's final assessment: "All in all, Mr Coombs has produced a most exhilarating vehicle, practical, purposeful and potent."

Even at this time the Coombs workforce were not fully conversant with the plans to 'publicise' the car and no special preparations were made to increase production. As it was, very little happened, there was no influx of new orders for modified cars and it appears no further publicity took place. The Cotswold Blue demonstrator was used by the company for a while and then sold – does the car still exist?

Turning now to the Coombs brochure, the introduction is worth repeating:

"The Jaguar 3.4 and 3.8 litre Mark II cars are fast, safe and complete in standard form, but we are able to offer discerning motorists even better performance and handling resulting in virtually a full 5-seater Grand Touring car at moderate cost.

Modification can be effected on either new or used cars and one of the significant points is that the cars still retain their outstanding flexibility.

Experience gained through many years of racing and servicing these cars is inbuilt in the modifications offered and we shall be pleased to discuss customers' individual requirements and arrange for a demonstration in a fully modified car."

Coombs obviously appreciated that the standard cars were excellent in their own right, and were keen to ensure their modifications would not affect the smoothness or flexibility of the cars.

The extra fuel tank was fitted behind the rear seat.

Coombs modifications were split up into three categories. The first was:

The Basic Conversion

Item	Price
To removing engine and gearbox from chassis, dismantling engine, fitting 9 to 1 compression pistons, specially balancing crankshaft, conrods and clutch assembly, fitting lightened flywheel, dismantling cylinder head for full gas flowing and attention to manifold and valve seats. Fitting open trumpet carburettor intakes. Re-assembling all parts and re-installing engine unit into chassis. Running engine, testing and tuning.	**£185**
Supplying and fitting new high ratio steering box giving 3½ turns lock to lock.	**£20**
Making up and fitting cold air intake to carburettors complete with polished air spreader.	**£35**
Supplying and fitting Vari-Flow adjustable shock absorbers all round.	**£17.10s**
Plus exhaust modifications:-	
(a) Supplying and fitting Servais silencers but retaining standard tail pipe.	**£11.11s**
(b) As in (a) but with modified tail pipes of straight through pattern.	**£21**
(c) As in (b) but with hand-made silencers.	**£28**
Maximum total cost for Basic Conversion:	**£285.10s**

Engine bay of a true Coombs car. Note the air duct to the carbs.

Of course, any one or permutation of the above modifications could be specified without the need to purchase the whole package. This also applied to the following two categories of conversion.

Further Specialist Items

Modified rear wheel arches deleting valances

(a) Normal body colours	£35
(b) Special colours and opalescents	£45
Leather covered roof panel, choice of colours	£49.10s
A.S.M. Chromium boot rack	£14
Additional long range 9.4 gallon fuel tank (fitted in front end of boot compartment with separate filler)	£62.10s
Supplying and fitting E Type woodrim steering wheel with centre horn push	£15
Wire wheel conversion (a) new cars	£42.5s.10d
(b) used cars	£100
Chromium plated wire wheels (a) new cars	£93.12s.11d
(b) used cars	£138
Manually controlled choke switch	£1.10s

Further items for competition motorists

Cylinder head machined to give 9.5 to 1 compression ratio in conjunction with basic conversion – extra charge	£4.10s
H.D8 2″ S.U. carburettor conversion in conjunction with basic conversion – extra cost	£40
Strengthened rear spring location	£10
High rate front springs	£14
Special anti-roll bar	£10

364 DLD, a genuine Coombs car still racing today.

The full conversion could cost over £600 on top of the normal purchase price for a 3.8 litre Mark II of £1,556. A one-third increase in the price of any car would put a lot of people off, but on the price of an already successful and fast car like the Mark II it may well have made Jaguar owners think twice about such expense. However, the performance figures quoted by Coombs for their modified 3.8 were quite outstanding. The following figures were based on contemporary *Autocar* road-test figures for the standard 3.8 litre Mark II saloon and E Type sports car. The Coombs car figures were apparently taken by Coombs themselves.

From rest through the gears to:	Standard 3.8 MkII	Coombs 3.8 with std. carbs.	Coombs 3.8 with 2″ carbs.	Standard E Type 3.8
30mph	3.2 sec.	2.2 sec.	2.2 sec.	2.8 sec.
40mph	4.9 sec.	3.4 sec.	3.3 sec.	4.4 sec.
50mph	6.4 sec.	5.3 sec.	5.1 sec.	5.6 sec.
60mph	8.5 sec.	7.3 sec.	7.0 sec.	6.9 sec.
70mph	11.7 sec.	10.0 sec.	8.2 sec.	8.5 sec.
80mph	14.6 sec.	12.0 sec.	12.1 sec.	11.1 sec.
90mph	18.2 sec.	15.3 sec.	13.4 sec.	13.2 sec.
100mph	25.1 sec.	18.3 sec.	16.2 sec.	16.2 sec.
110mph	33.2 sec.	23.0 sec.	20.4 sec.	19.2 sec.
Standing ¼ mile	16.3 sec.	15.81 sec.	15.72 sec.	14.7 sec.

Quite amazing figures, I think you will agree. Faster than an E Type to 50mph and as fast to 100! Even compared with modern-day supercars the Coombs Mark II still has the edge. And, what is more, Coombs appeared to get it right first time, there being no real prototype or testing period. They took great pains to ensure the engine and all components were accurately balanced and at no time saw the necessity to delve further into bored out blocks, triple carburettors or the like. I have heard it said that the Coombs modified cars were not only faster but also much smoother than the standard cars, that the engines were actually under less stress, and above all that they were totally reliable.

Very few of the forty cars were modified to the maximum, in fact only about ten including Coombs' own racers. A further ten or so had the full Coombs engine treatment with modified 2″ carburettors, and even fewer had the modified springs. Apart from the strictly competition cars, only about two others are known to have had bucket seats fitted but all cars had the strengthened rear end which involved the welding of ⅛″ plate across the floor pan. All cars ran on standard production type car tyres.

Ram air ducting to the front brakes was an extra modification only fitted to the BUY 12s and the old 3.4 (TWK 287), and what is most interesting is the myth that the louvred bonnet was a standard Coombs modification. This is not true, and apart from the demonstration model 7 YPG, the louvred bonnet was only known to have been fitted to perhaps one or two cars, entirely at the customers' request. The louvred bonnet was never listed by Coombs as a modification. Another little anecdote concerns the fitment of the E Type woodrim steering wheel, which apparently was done on nearly all the cars modified. In most cases the standard E Type steering wheel centre boss was used, but on a couple of cars an attempt was made to re-fit the normal Mark II steering wheel badge. To do this, non-vented Mark II petrol filler caps were used, suitably cut to size and drilled to fit!

As Coombs & Sons (Guildford) have kept no records of their own relating

*364 DLD also has the genuinely
modified rear wheel arches, made
up with brass tubing.*

to the modified Mark I and IIs and are not even Jaguar distributors now, I hope
my few words have helped to put the record straight, confirming or disproving
the many rumours and legends attached to these cars. They were a special
breed of Jaguar and if ever the opportunity arises to purchase one of the 'real'
cars, take the bull by the horns – but beware the fakes!

After the exciting Coombs Mark IIs, could there possibly be anything
more appealing or exotic? How about a pure gold Mark II? Yes, Jaguar had a
rather special 3.8 saloon prepared for the 1960 New York Motor Show in the
form of a white car with white upholstery, white-wall tyres and, to replace the
ordinary chromium plate, real gold used extensively, even on the wire wheels!
The car cost an estimated five times the price of a standard 3.8 litre automatic.
Little is known of the car but all the gold fittings were removed and replaced by
chrome before the car was sold. Does this remind anyone of the Docker
Daimlers?

Not too many of the older well-known Mark IIs still exist. We have already
covered the ex-factory car 1628 VC but should mention that the present owner
Tim Spital has acquired an old Mark I for parts and is busy investigating the
whereabouts of the original engine. The unit fitted during production was
replaced before the factory sold the car in the first place. An interesting
rumour exists about this car. Apparently the garage that supplied the car wrote
off a customer's competition Mark II whilst road-testing it, the customer being
John Sparrow. The garage were extremely embarrassed by the episode so the
managing director (who had very good connections with the factory)
contacted Browns Lane to see what they could do to get him out of his
predicament. The factory came up with 1628 VC! Only conjecture but an
interesting little story.

Another VC registered Mark II reputedly still exists, that being 7116 VC,
the ex-Monza record breaking car.

None of the original factory demonstrators or show cars are apparently
still around but quite a few very early models still exist. I am given to
understand that a 2.4 litre Mark II of single figure chassis number rests in a
scrapyard in the south of England, supposedly complete with its original Mark
I radiator grille. Several other cars with early chassis numbers from No. 175
onwards are still in good health and running. Perhaps one of the more
important early cars is the November 1959 3.8 Mark II which used to belong to
Bruce McLaren. He owned the car until 1963, taking the car with him to New

Zealand in 1961. From 1963 to 1970 the car belonged to Les McLaren and is now in the hands of a Jaguar enthusiast out there who has restored it. Apparently standard except for wire wheels and 9 to 1 compression engine, the car is still in remarkable condition.

An interesting project, not directly associated with the factory, was carried out in the early sixties on a 3.8 litre Mark II, which was converted into an estate car. The idea was originally thought up by Mike Hawthorn but never came to fruition due to his death. The concept was, however, taken up and produced as a one-off by Jones Bros (Coachbuilders) Limited, and the car was subsequently used by the factory, first as a team support vehicle carrying spares, tyres, etc. around the rallies and circuits of Europe and then later as a general hack vehicle delivering bits and pieces between Radford and Browns Lane. Mike McDowell, Ted Brooks and Andrew Whyte all used to drive the estate known as the 'County'.

The County was quite professionally built and utilised the then popular concept of two half tail-gates, one opening upwards, the lower half folding down. Preempting the possibility of producing the car commercially, the Jones company even affixed a 'County' badge to the tail-gate. Although quite professionally done, the estate conversion was not without its faults. Ineffective sealing was a constant problem, causing water leaks and more importantly the admission of exhaust fumes sucked up by the revised body shape. Otherwise the car was well finished. The upper chrome-rimmed tail-gate was hand-made for the car whilst the bottom tail-gate was made up from the existing boot lid, even retaining the old boot lock, although this was superfluous. Interior trim including wood cappings was continued to the luggage section. Mechanically the car was apparently standard 3.8 although I understand that one weekend some of the Jaguar apprentices got hold of the car and 'tweaked' it sufficiently to make it 'go like hell', in the words of an ex-factory employee who drove the car afterwards!

The County, registered 3672 VC, eventually left factory ownership and generally deteriorated badly but it was still running when purchased by John Pearson (of racing fame). John did not, however, carry out any work on the car and ownership passed on to a Midlands gentleman who had it totally restored and converted to wire wheels. Apparently in concours condition, 3672VC was then advertised a couple of times through the major motoring magazines in 1977/78 for around £3,000 and was subsequently sold and sent to America. Contrary to belief there was only one Mark II estate and not two or three.

During the sixties the police were very impressed with Jaguar's Mark II saloons. Many constabularies moved on to Mark IIs after a successful period with Mark Is. Others changed over to Jaguars from other makes, especially those police authorities responsible for motorway patrol. The 3.8 Mark II was 'made to measure' for motorway work, with performance to match most other cars on the road, driver comfort for long-distance driving, reliability in service and reasonable economy when driven for long periods at steady speeds in overdrive top. At one time no less than thirty-seven police authorities used Mark IIs in various capacities. Some cars were retained in standard Jaguar colours as unmarked vehicles, others were retained in standard colours but utilised police signs and stickers, but the majority were specially ordered with quite extensive modification.

Some Police authorities went to town by specifying a total modification package on all cars, others had only minor changes made, and some were totally standard cars in all respects. The ultimate police version Mark II was modified as follows:

Exterior
Paint finish usually conventional Old English White although some authorities specified Arctic White or similar, later a standardised 'special colour' for police vehicles only. At front of vehicle addition of twin tone 14" Fiamm chrome air horns (compressor under bonnet), bumper mounted loudhailer and wing mirrors.

*Mark II 3.8 litre Police cars
purchased in 1965 by Staffordshire
County Constabulary.*

*Staffordshire Police later acquired
some 240s.*

Door sides featured either fluorescent POLICE lettering or bright orange fluorescent panel with POLICE lettering attached.

From the rear the only appreciable difference was the addition of two high-intensity red flashing lights and a POLICE sticker on the boot lid.

Mechanics
Contrary to popular opinion virtually all police equipped Mark IIs had the standard 3.8 litre engine and gearbox although high-output dynamos were always fitted and in some cases uprated springs were specified. Kenlowe electric fans were also featured on some cars.

Interior
Usually the rear seat was replaced by numerous metal brackets to hold firm various signs, cones, flashing lights and other roadside equipment. Front seating was standard, with double lap and diagonal seat belts. In some cases door panels and door cappings were replaced by plain black painted hardboard panelling. The headlining remained intact although with switches handy to the driver and passenger to operate the blue flashing light, POLICE and POLICE STOP signs on the roof. Radio telephones were fitted either to the dashboard or to the passenger side of the centre transmission tunnel. Dashboards were usually standard except for the removal of the glove-box lid to make room for the radio-telephone controls and/or the fitment of a separate highly accurate speedometer calibrated to 140mph. Alternatively this extra speedometer would be situated at the head of the transmission tunnel, angled towards the passenger. Again, as with the door panels, in some cases dashboards would be finished in matt black to stop glare. The only other addition was the fitment of an extra rear-view mirror.

The height of Mark II police involvement was from late 1962 to early 1966. The Jaguars were well liked by the drivers, one passing the comment to me, "I loved driving the Jags. As well as comfortable, they were exhilarating".

With the demise of the Mark II in 1967 many police authorities changed to BMWs, Ford Zodiacs and the like until the XJ6 was established. Some authorities, however, remained faithful to Jaguars, utilising the 240 model in normal guise but with similar police modifications to those mentioned above. Spot lights were standardised for the police vehicles and in some cases bonnet mascots were not fitted. Very rarely were 340s supplied to the police, the authorities obviously being well pleased with the performance of the 240. One supposed that with improved communications and experience gained on the motorways, out and out speed was no longer that important – road blocks being more in favour to stop the spirited E Type driver!

Finally there are the very important concours cars. The concours is a very important and worthwhile feature of the Jaguar clubs' activities. Until a few years ago the concours was the domain of the pre-war cars, XKs and latterly E Types. Now the Mark I and II have a firm hold on the concours scene and there are quite a few examples of the model series in what can only be described as better than new condition. Originality is important, not only from the pure concours competition point of view but more importantly to ensure the survival of some cars to production specification. It can be argued that Jaguar 'got it right' with the standad production models and that there is no need for modification.

Let us now look at some of the more unusual modified Mark IIs still around. In the seventies Alfie Betts produced three or four Mark II 'Mulsannes' or in other words Mark IIs with 5.4 litre Chevrolet engines! These cars were hairy to say the least and apparently kicked up a terrible noise when started. The conversion was apparently well done but the standard Mark II braking system was retained. One of the cars is now in a private collection, the whereabouts of the others are unknown.

Also in the late seventies, someone converted a Mark II into a pick-up. Eventually painted in black with gold coachlines, the car became known as

Highly modified 3.8 litre engine
with triple 2" SU carburettors
necessitating the revised siting of
brake master cylinder, etc.

the 'Tandberg' apparently because the owner ran a hi-fi shop selling Tandberg equipment. Well finished, the pick-up featured Wolfrace wheels, chrome engine parts, front spoilers and a very neatly executed rear loading area, complete with canvas top. This vehicle has now dropped out of club circles but was apparently seen not long ago in the High Wycombe area.

The 'Tandberg' Mark II-based pick-up, a conversion carried out in the late seventies.

A most unusual Mark II, fitted with a Perkins diesel engine!

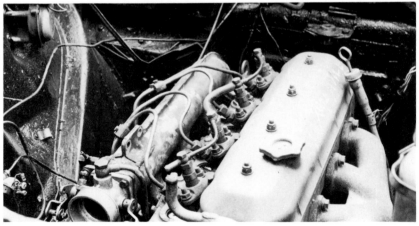

The most unusual Mark II around must be the recently built two door convertible produced by a Mr Waterman of Kent to his own specification. The car was originally a Daimler 2.5 V8 from 1963. Mechanically the car now has a modified 2.4 litre Mark I engine, wide wheels and stiffened suspension.

Mr Waterman had always been a fan of the open car and decided to plan and build his own Mark II-based convertible. The car took two years to build and apart from the hood, all work was carried out by Mr Waterman himself.

Standard Mark II front doors were used, without the chromium window frames (although retaining the quarter-lights). The rear doors were

The exciting and practical
Copycats C Type replica built
around Mark II mechanicals.

abandoned and door skins were welded into place. To provide sufficient strength the outer sills were removed and reinforced round section tubing was welded in along the whole floor pan area; the outer sills were then replaced and thus the reinforcement was entirely out of sight. To further prevent flexing of the body, square box sections were welded on to the floor pan transversely.

The standard Mark II windscreen was retained along with 3″ of the roof section. An extensively modified Triumph Herald hood frame was utilised, retrimmed with side screens. The hood folds completely out of sight behind the rear seat and into wells in the welded-in rear door skins. To allow the hood to fold away completely the boot had to be modified, moving the hinges 8″ further back and losing the front 8″ of the boot area.

The dashboard is standard Mark II except that most of it is leather covered, leaving the centre section finished in wood veneer (à la Mark X). A centre console is also fitted. Front seats are modified NSU items and the back seat also came from an NSU Prinz, the centre 8″ being cut out, the seat rejoined and retrimmed, allowing room for the hood mechanism at the sides.

The conversion is very well thought out although not to everyone's taste. But if one likes the Mark II, why not modify it to one's own personal requirements?

Lastly, perhaps one of the most popular conversions on the Mark II today is the Copycats C Type replica. This car, produced on a very small scale, is hand made in Bolton, Lancashire. Based on the principle of utilising Mark II mechanicals from a rusted out shell, the car quite closely follows the lines of the famous racing C Types of the early fifties, and utilises a tubular steel spaceframe to the same layout as the original C Type. The bodywork consists of a hand-crafted aluminium central hull section and doors, with bonnet and tail sections of high quality G.R.P., although all louvred panels are in aluminium. Apart from the specially designed seats and fuel tank, all other items are modified from the Mark II including the C Type replica radiator grille.

The Copycats C Type replica can be supplied as a built up complete car or as a kit. After driving the prototype some time ago I have to admit to being impressed by the overall solidity of the structure. The car is very quick, certainly an eye-catcher and proved great fun to drive. The replica provides the sight and sound of the C Type but at affordable Mark II prices and is another way of keeping Mark IIs on the road long after their original bodies have deteriorated beyond recovery.

overleaf

The Waterman convertible, an
alluring and beautifully finished
car based on a 1963 Daimler V8.
It is now fitted with a modified
2.4 litre engine.

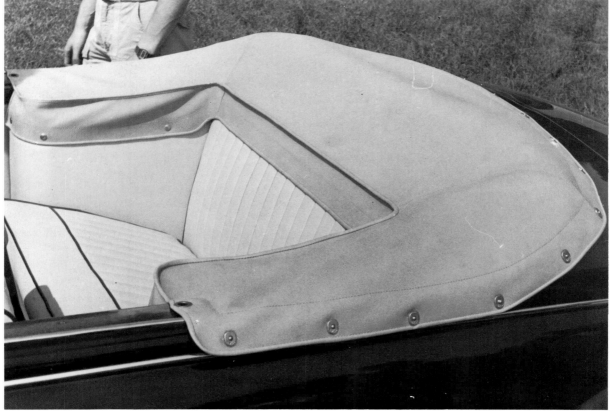

Specifications and Production Details

In the following pages the reader will find a breakdown of production figures for the cars covered in the book along with detailed specifications for each individual model. Any road-test figures given are taken from contemporary road-test reports, which tended to vary slightly from car to car and magazine to magazine.

Mark I 2.4 litre

Number of cylinders		6
Bore		83mm
Stroke		76.5mm
Cubic capacity		2,483cc
RAC Rating		25.6hp
Compression ratio		7:1 or 8:1
Maximum bhp		112 at 5,750rpm
Carburettors		2 Solex downdraught
Rear axle ratio	Without overdrive	4.27:1
	With overdrive	4.55:1
	Automatic	4.27:1
Tyres		6.40x15
Wheelbase		8'11⅜"
Track Cars with drum brakes		4'6⅝" front
		4'2⅛" rear
Cars with disc brakes		4'7⅛" front
		4'2⅜" rear
Overall length		15'0¾"
Overall width		5'6¾"
Overall height		4'9½"
Dry weight		25cwt
Turning circle		33'6"
Ground clearance		7"
Braking system		Lockheed Brakemaster drum, servo assisted, or Dunlop disc
Steering		Burman recirculating ball
Transmission		Borg & Beck dry plate clutch, Moss 4 speed gearbox
Gearbox ratios 1st		15.35
2nd		9.01
3rd		6.21
4th		4.55
Front suspension		Independent, helical springs and wishbones. Anti-roll bar
Rear suspension		Cantilevered live axle, radius arms, Panhard rod, half elliptic leaf springs
Shock absorbers		Girling telescopic

Performance data

0 to 30mph	4.6 seconds
0 to 40mph	6.9 seconds
0 to 50mph	11 seconds
0 to 60mph	14.4 seconds
0 to 70mph	19.9 seconds
0 to 80mph	28.6 seconds
0 to 90mph	39.1 seconds
Standing quarter mile	24.6 seconds

Maximum speed	101.5mph
Maximum speeds in gears	
1st	28mph
2nd	47mph
3rd	68.5mph
4th	93.5mph

Overall fuel consumption	18.3mpg

Production details

2.4 public release, September 1955

First rhd car completed at Browns Lane on 7th January 1955, chassis number 900001 with engine number BB1002/8. This car was finished in black with red interior and was later dismantled, having been built for experimental purposes.

Chassis number 900002 with engine number BB1001/8 Birch Grey
Chassis number 900003 with engine number BB1003/8 Pastel Blue
Chassis number 900004 with engine number BB1005/8 Black
Chassis number 900005 with engine number BB1007/8 Grey

All the above cars were also experimental and were subsequently dismantled except for chassis 900004 which, although scrapped, had its engine and registration number transferred to chassis number 903326, better known as PVC 302, works demonstrator.

The first true production car which survived as such was chassis number 900007 with engine number BB1011/8, registered RVC 592, finished in Pearl Grey with blue interior and invoiced to Henley's as a demonstrator on 11th October 1955. The very last 2.4 litre saloon produced in rhd form was chassis number 916250 with engine number BE2967/8, completed on 28th August 1959, finished in Pearl Grey with red interior and registered PVH 592.

Left hand drive 2.4s commenced at chassis number 940001, this particular car being completed on 21st November 1955 with engine number BB1023/8 and finished in Green with red interior. It was subsequently shipped to Jaguar's New York distributors as a demonstrator. The very last lhd car was chassis number 943742 with engine number BE2341/8, finished in Green with red interior and carrying the English registration number 3087 DU.

Mark 1 2.4 litre cars total production was 16149 rhd, 3741 lhd.

Mark 1 3.4 litre

Number of cylinders	6
Bore	83mm
Stroke	106mm
Cubic capacity	3,442cc
RAC rating	25.6hp
Compression ratio	7:1 or 8:1

Maximum bhp		210 at 5,500rpm
Carburettors		2 1¾" SU HD6
Rear axle ratio	Without overdrive	3.54:1
	With overdrive	3.77:1
	Automatic	3.54:1
Tyres		6.40x15
Wheelbase		8'11⅜"
Track		4'6⅝" front
		4'2" rear
Overall length		15'0¾"
Overall width		5'6¾"
Overall height		4'9½"
Dry weight		25cwt
Turning circle		33'6"
Ground clearance		7"
Braking system		Dunlop disc
Steering		Burman recirculating ball
Transmission		Borg & Beck dry plate clutch, Moss 4 speed gearbox
Gearbox ratios 1st		11.2
2nd		6.56
3rd		4.55
4th		3.77
Front suspension		Independent, coil spring and wishbone. Anti-roll bar
Rear suspension		Cantilevered live axle, radius arms, Panhard rod, half elliptic leaf springs
Shock absorbers		Girling telescopic
Performance data		
0 to 30mph		3.6 seconds
0 to 40mph		6.0 seconds
0 to 50mph		8.0 seconds
0 to 60mph		10.0 seconds
0 to 70mph		14.3 seconds
0 to 80mph		18.0 seconds
0 to 90mph		22.1 seconds
Standing quarter mile		17.9 seconds
Maximum speed		119.8mph
Maximum speeds in gears		
1st		36mph *
2nd		67mph
3rd		97mph
4th		119.8mph
Overall fuel consumption		16mpg

Production details
3.4 public release, end of February 1957.

First rhd car completed at Browns Lane on 27th December 1956, chassis number 970001 with engine number KE.1015/8. This car was finished in Cornish Grey with red interior and was registered UDU 94 – no further history is known. The very next car, chassis number 970002 with engine number KE.1024/8, was registered THP 677, used temporarily by the factory and then sold on to John Coombs of Guildford.

The very last 3.4 litre Mark I produced in right hand drive form was chassis number 978946 with engine number KF.7851/8, finished in British Racing Green with suede interior, completed on 28th August 1959, other history unkown. Left hand drive 3.4s commenced at chassis number 985001, the first car being completed on 24th October 1956, with engine number KE.1001/8, finished in Red with black interior and shipped out to Jaguar in North America. The very last left hand drive 3.4 was chassis number 993460 with engine number KF.9044, finished in British Racing Green with suede interior completed on 15th September 1959 but subsequently converted to right hand drive under chassis number 978924 and then registered 3253 DU. The last true left hand drive car was then chassis number 993459 with engine number KF.9325/9, finished in Cotswold Blue with blue interior,completed on 9th September 1959 and despatched via Liverpool docks to a Mr Hoffman of Mobile, Alabama.

Mark 1 3.4 litre cars total production was 8945rhd, 8459lhd.

Mark II 2.4 litre

Number of cylinders		6
Bore		83mm
Stroke		76.5mm
Cubic capacity		2,483cc
RAC rating		25.6hp
Compression ratio		7:1 or 8:1
Maximum bhp		120 at 5,750rpm
Carburettors		2 Solex downdraught
Rear axle ratio	Without overdrive	4.27:1
	With overdrive	4.55:1
	Automatic	4.27:1
Tyres		6.40x15
Wheelbase		8'11¼"
Track		4'7" front
		4'5⅜" rear
Overall length		15'0¾"
Overall width		5'6¾"
Overall height		4'9¾"
Dry weight		28.5cwt
Turning circle		33'6"
Braking system		Dunlop disc
Steering		Burman recirculating ball
Transmission		Borg & Beck dry plate clutch, Moss 4 speed gearbox
Gearbox ratios 1st		14.42
2nd		7.94
3rd		5.48
4th		4.27
Front suspension		Independent, coil springs, wishbones and anti-roll bar
Rear suspension		Cantilevered live axle, radius arms, Panhard rod, half elliptic leaf springs
Shock absorbers		Girling telescopic
Performance data		
0 to 30mph		5.7 seconds
0 to 40mph		8.5 seconds

0 to 50mph	12.7 seconds
0 to 60mph	17.3 seconds
0 to 70mph	23.8 seconds
0 to 80mph	33.3 seconds
0 to 90mph	49.9 seconds
Standing quarter mile	20.8 seconds
Maximum speed	96.3mph
Maximum speeds in gears	
1st	26mph
2nd	49mph
3rd	69mph
4th	96mph
Overall fuel consumption	18mpg

Production details

Mark II 2.4 public release, September 1959.

First rhd car completed at Browns Lane on 20th August 1959, chassis number 100001, engine number BG.1001/8, finished in Maroon with grey interior, registered GCA 42 and sold in Luton, Bedfordshire. The second car was the original demonstrator model, chassis number 100002 with engine number BG.1003/8, registered on 1st September 1959 in Cotswold Blue with grey interior. The very last 2.4 litre right hand drive car produced was chassis number 121769. Left hand drive 2.4 Mark IIs commenced at chassis number 125001 with engine number BG.1004/8, this particular car being released from the factory on 25th August 1959, finished in Cotswold Blue with grey interior, despatched to Nice. The very last left hand drive 2.4 was chassis number 128405DN with engine number BJ.8090-8, released on 4th July 1967, finished in British Racing Green with tan leather interior.

Mark II 2.4 litre cars total production was 21768 rhd, 3405 lhd.

Mark II 3.4 litre.

Number of cylinders		6
Bore		83mm
Stroke		106mm
Cubic capacity		3,442cc
RAC rating		25.6hp
Compression ratio		7:1, 8:1 or 9:1
Maximum bhp		210 at 5,500rpm
Carburettors		2 1¾″ SU HD6
Rear axle ratio	Without overdrive	3.54:1
	With overdrive	3.77:1
	Automatic	3.54:1
Tyres		6.40x15
Wheelbase		8′11⅜″
Track		4′7″ front
		4′5⅜″ rear
Overall length		15′0¾″
Overall width		5′6¾″
Overall height		4′9¾″
Dry weight		29.25cwt
Turning circle		33′6″
Braking system		Dunlop disc

Steering	Burman recirculating ball, optional power assistance
Transmission	Borg & Beck dry plate clutch, Moss 4 speed gearbox
Gearbox ratios 1st	11.95
2nd	6.58
3rd	4.54
4th	3.54
Front suspension	Independent, coil springs, wishbones and anti-roll bar
Rear suspension	Cantilevered live axle, radius arms, Panhard rod, half elliptic leaf springs
Shock absorbers	Girling telescopic
Performance data	
0 to 30mph	4.5 seconds
0 to 40mph	6.4 seconds
0 to 50mph	9.0 seconds
0 to 60mph	11.9 seconds
0 to 70mph	15.9 seconds
0 to 80mph	20.0 seconds
0 to 90mph	26.0 seconds
0 to 100mph	33.3 seconds
0 to 110mph	44.5 seconds
Standing quarter mile	19.1 seconds
Maximum speed	119.9mph
Maximum speeds in gears	(automatic transmission model only tested)
Overall fuel consumption	16mpg (automatic)

Production details

Mark II 3.4 first public release, October 1959.

First right hand drive car, chassis number 150001 with engine number KG.1001/8, was completed on 15th July 1959, finished in Indigo Blue with grey interior, registered XYH 348 and supplied to the Westinghouse Brake & Signal Company by Henleys of London. The very last right hand drive 3.4 was chassis number 172095, engine number KJ.11587/8, completed on 21st August 1967 in Willow Green with tan interior, and was initially supplied to Quick Tools Ltd., of Portsmouth. The first left hand drive chassis produced was number 175001, completed on 3rd September 1959 with engine number KG.1073/8, finished in Pearl Grey with black interior and wire wheels. The last 3.4 left hand drive car produced was chassis number 181571BW with engine number KG.1153-8, released on 21st August 1967, finished in Golden Sand with tan trim, registered NDU 666F and supplied to a Mr Beeley of Geneva.

Mark II 3.4 litre total production was 22092 rhd, 6571 lhd.

Mark II 3.8 litre

Number of cylinders	6
Bore	87mm
Stroke	106mm
Cubic capacity	3,781cc
RAC rating	25.6hp

Compression ratio		7:1, 8:1 or 9:1
Maximum bhp		220 at 5,500rpm
Carburettors		2 1¾" SU HD6
Rear axle ratio	Without overdrive	3.54:1
	With overdrive	3.77:1
	Automatic	3.54:1
Tyres		6.40x15
Wheelbase		8'11⅜"
Track		4'7" front
		4'5⅜" rear
Overall length		15'0¾"
Overall width		5'6¾"
Overall height		4'9¾"
Dryweight		29.25cwt
Turning circle		33'6"
Braking system		Dunlop disc
Steering		Burman recirculating ball, optional power assistance
Transmission		Borg & Beck dry plate clutch, Moss 4 speed gearbox
Gearbox ratios	1st	11.95
	2nd	6.58
	3rd	4.54
	4th	3.54
Front suspension		Independent, coil springs, wishbones and anti-roll bar
Rear suspension		Cantilevered live axle, radius arms, Panhard rod, half elliptic leaf springs
Shock absorbers		Girling telescopic

Performance data		
0 to 30mph		3.2 seconds
0 to 40mph		4.9 seconds
0 to 50mph		6.4 seconds
0 to 60mph		8.5 seconds
0 to 70mph		11.7 seconds
0 to 80mph		14.6 seconds
0 to 90mph		18.2 seconds
0 to 100mph		25.1 seconds
0 to 110mph		33.2 seconds
Standing quarter mile		16.3 seconds
Maximum speed		126mph
Maximum speeds in gears	1st	35mph
	2nd	64mph
	3rd	98mph
	4th	120mph
Overall fuel consumption		15.7mpg

Production details

The 3.8 was released to the public along with the other Mark IIs in October 1959. The very first chassis number was 200001 with engine number LA.1285/8, completed on 18th September 1959 in British Racing Green with green interior, registered YHP 790 and used by the factory as a demonstration car. The very last 3.8 right hand drive was chassis number 235383 with engine number LE.4270/8, completed on 22nd September 1967. This car was finished in Golden Sand with red interior and had leather upholstery.

Left hand drive 3.8 Mark IIs commenced at chassis number 210001 with engine number LA 601/8, finished in Cornish Grey with grey interior and registered 200 HP. This car was kept by Jaguar and converted to right hand drive on 19th February 1960. The first exported 3.8 was chassis number 210003 with engine number LA.1002/8, finished in Cornish Grey with grey interior and sent to Princetown, New Jersey. The very last 3.8 Mark II left hand drive was released from the factory on 29th August 1967, chassis number 224758 with engine number LE.4230/8, finished in Golden Sand with tan leather interior.

Mark II 3.8 total production was 15383 rhd, 14757 lhd.

240

Number of cylinders	6
Bore	83mm
Stroke	76.5mm
Cubic capacity	2,483cc
RAC rating	25.6hp
Compression ratio	8:1
Maximum bhp	133 at 5,500rpm
Carburettors	2 1¾" SU HS6
Rear axle ratios Without overdrive	4.27:1
With overdrive	4.55:1
Automatic	4.27:1
Tyres	6.40x15
Wheelbase	8'11⅜"
Track	4'7" front
	4'5⅜" rear
Overall length	15'0⅜"
Overall width	5'6¾"
Overall height	4'9½"
Dry weight	26.5cwt
Turning circle	33'6"
Braking system	Dunlop disc
Steering	Burman recirculating ball
Transmission	Dry plate clutch,
	4 speed all-synchro gearbox
Gearbox ratios 1st	12.19
2nd	7.93
3rd	5.78
4th	4.55
Front suspension	Independent, coil springs,
	wishbones and anti-roll bar
Rear suspension	Cantilevered live axle,
	radius arms, Panhard rod,
	half elliptic leaf springs
Shock absorbers	Girling telescopic

Performance data

0 to 30mph	4.1	seconds
0 to 40mph	6.3	seconds
0 to 50mph	9.3	seconds

0 to 60mph	12.5 seconds
0 to 70mph	16.4 seconds
0 to 80mph	22.8 seconds
0 to 90mph	31.0 seconds
0 to 100mph	44.8 seconds
Standing quarter mile	18.7 seconds
Maximum speed	106mph
Maximum speeds in gears 1st	35mph
2nd	63mph
3rd	73mph
4th	106mph
Overall fuel consumption	18.4mpg

Production details

The 240 was released to the public in September 1967. The very first chassis number was 1J1001 ON, right hand drive, released from the factory on 23rd June 1967 with engine number 7J.1037-8, finished in Cream with dark blue trim. The last right hand drive car was chassis number 1J.4716DN with engine number 7J.5419-8, released on 9th April 1969, finished in British Racing Green with black trim, sold to a Mr Brossard of London. The first left hand drive car was chassis number 1J.30001DN with engine number 7J.1087-8, released on 18th August 1967, finished in Cream with red leather interior, and exported to Spain. The last left hand drive car was 1J.30730DN, with engine number 7J.4510-8, released on 11th March 1969, going to Holland, finished in Sable with beige leather interior.

240 total production was 3716 rhd, 730 lhd.

340

Number of cylinders	6
Bore	83mm
Stroke	106mm
Cubic capacity	3,442cc
RAC rating	25.6hp
Compression ratio	7:1 or 8:1
Maximum bhp	210 at 5,500rpm
Carburettors	2 1¾" SU HD6
Rear axle ratio Without overdrive	3.54:1
With overdrive	3.77:1
Automatic	3.54:1
Tyres	640x15
Wheelbase	8'11⅜"
Track	4'7" front
	4'5⅜" rear
Overall length	15'0⅜"
Overall width	5'6¾"
Overall height	4'9½"
Dry weight	30cwt
Turning circle	33'6"
Braking system	Dunlop disc
Steering	Burman recirculating ball, optional power assistance
Transmission	Dry plate clutch, 4 speed all-synchro gearbox

Gearbox ratios	1st	12.73
	2nd	7.012
	3rd	4.83
	4th	3.77
Front suspension		Independent, coil springs, wishbones, anti-roll bar
Rear suspension		Cantilevered live axle, radius arms, Panhard rod, Half elliptic leaf springs
Shock absorbers		Girling telescopic

Performance data

0 to 30mph	3.5 seconds
0 to 50mph	6.9 seconds
0 to 60mph	8.8 seconds
0 to 80mph	16.6 seconds
0 to 100mph	26.4 seconds
Standing quarter mile	17.2 seconds
Maximum speed	124mph

Maximum speeds in gears	1st	36mph
	2nd	60mph
	3rd	85mph
	4th	115mph
Overall fuel consumption		17.22mpg

Production Details

The 340 was released to the public in September 1967 and the first right hand drive chassis number was 1J.50001 with engine number 7J.50121-8, finished in Dark Blue with red leather interior and registered LDU 853F. The car was completed on 23rd June 1967 and used by Jaguar themselves. The last 340 right hand drive car had chassis number 1J.52265BW with engine number 7J.50379-8, released on 29th August 1968, finished in Black with beige Ambla trim. This car was registered TDD 412G and was sold to English Rose Kitchens Limited of Warwick. Left hand drive 340s began at chassis number 1J.80001 and terminated at number 1J.80535BW with engine number 7J.52788-8, this particular car registered NKV 711G and finished in Cream with Red Ambla interior.

340 total production 2265 rhd, 535 lhd.

Daimler 2½ litre V8 and V8 250 saloons.

Number of cylinders	8
Bore	76.2mm
Stroke	69.85mm
Cubic capacity	2,548cc
Compression ratio	8.2:1
Carburettors	Twin SU
Rear axle ratio	4.27:1
Tyres	640x15
Wheelbase	8'11⅜"
Track	4'7" front
	4'5⅜" rear
Overall length	15'0⅜"

Overall width	5′6¾″
Overall height	4′9½″
Dry weight	26½cwt
Turning circle	33′6″
Steering	Burman recirculating ball
Transmission	Borg Warner automatic (Manual option later)

Production details

The V8 Daimler model was released to the public in the autumn of 1962 and the very first right hand drive car produced was chassis number 1A 1001 with engine number 97331, registered 7792 VC and finished in opalescent Maroon with beige leather interior. This car was registered in November 1962 and was the original Earls Court motor show car. The first left hand drive model was on chassis number 1A 20001 with engine number 741100, released in December of 1962, finished in opalescent Dark Blue with grey interior and exported to Milan.

Production of V8 250s began in July 1967 and the first right hand drive model was on chassis number 1K1001BW with engine number 7A13670. The car was finished in Warwick Grey with red leather interior. The very last right hand drive Daimler produced was chassis number 1K 5780BW with engine number 7K5895 on 5th August 1969. This car was finished in Regency Red with beige leather trim, registered TCR 585H and sold to Vantage Photosetting of Southampton. The last left hand drive 2½ V8 produced was on 8th June 1967, chassis number 1A 20622DN with engine number 7A14081. The car was finished in opalescent Silver with dark blue interior and was registered NDU 658F, belonging to a Mr Neal of Canada. The very last Daimler (left hand drive) of all was on chassis number 1K 30105 DN with engine number 7K5417, released on 9th July 1969, finished in fawn with red interior.

Additional Material

Useful Addresses

Jaguar Cars Limited
Browns Lane, Allesley, Coventry, England

Clubs

Jaguar Enthusiasts' Club Limited
Sherborne Mead Road,
Stoke Gifford,
Bristol BS12 6TS
Membership Secretaries: Lynn and Graham Searle. Tel: 0272 698186

Jaguar Drivers' Club Limited
18 Stuart Street,
Luton,
Beds LU1 2SL
Secretary: Rosemary Hinton. Tel: 0582 419332

Jaguar Car Club
19 Eldorado Crescent,
Cheltenham,
Glos GL52 2PY
Secretary: Richard Pugh

As a very general guide to the clubs the JAGUAR ENTHUSIASTS' CLUB concentrates more on the practical side and technical advice for owners who drive and use their cars regularly. The J.E.C. offers many specialist services including spares and special tool remanufacture, telephone advice service, discounted insurance, etc. The JAGUAR CAR CLUB is the newest of the Jaguar marque clubs and concentrates on overseas trips, liaison with overseas Jaguar owners and enthusiasts, and competitive race activities. The JAGUAR DRIVERS' CLUB is the oldest established of the clubs and offers a wide range of outdoor events throughout the year.

Daimler & Lanchester Owners' Club
The Oak House,
Gamlingay,
Beds
Secretary: J. Ridley. Tel: 048 82563

The DAIMLER AND LANCHESTER OWNERS' CLUB, whilst traditionally involved with the older 'pre-Jaguar manufactured' models, now has a growing membership owning Jaguar-based cars including the V8 250 and 2.5-litre V8 models. The Club offers a fully equipped spares department for the use of members.

Jaguar Association of Germany
AMC Stemweder Berg e.V.im ADAC

Jaguar Drivers' Club Switzerland
Weissensteinstrasse, 15 Ch-4500, Solothurn
Secretary: Hans-Georg Kuny. Tel: 064 371414

Jaguar Daimler Club Holland
Zuider Kerkedijk 160,
Rotterdam
Secretary: F. Ferbrache. Tel: 010 821212

Jaguar Club Norway,
Postboks 1748 Vika,
0121 Oslo 1
Secretary: Jan L. Rodtwitt. Tel: 02 130257

Australian Council of Jaguar Clubs (Incorporating Jaguar Drivers' Club,
Newcastle, Jaguar Car Club of Victoria, Classic Jaguar Club of Western
Australia, Jaguar Driver Club of Western Australia, Jaguar Drivers' Club of
South Australia, Jaguar Car Club of Tasmania, Jaguar Drivers' Club of
Canberra, Jaguar Drivers' Club of Australia, Jaguar Drivers' Club of
Queensland)
4/87 Wellington Street,
Windsor,
Victoria 3181
Secretary: Alec Duke. Tel: 03 529 2022

There are numerous other Jaguar-orientated Clubs throughout the world
including a number in the USA.

Mark I/II Trade Specialists, Spares Suppliers etc.

David Manners Spares
Bell Barn,
991 Wolverhampton Road,
Oldbury, West Midlands B69 4RJ
Tel: 021 544 4040
(Complete range of new, remanufactured and secondhand parts, mechanical
and body, for Mark I/II and Daimlers)

Barry Hankinson
15 Copse Cross Street,
Ross-on-Wye,
Herefordshire HR9 5PB
Tel: 0989 65789
(Interior trim kits for Mark IIs)

M R Buckeridge Limited
Airedale Works,
Otley Road,
Shipley, West Yorks BD17 7SG
Tel: 0274 589389
(All types of mechanical work, body repairs and complete restorations on
all models)

Chris Coleman Spares
17 Devonshire Mews,
Chiswick,
London W4
Tel: 01 995 9833
(New and secondhand spares for all models)

M & C Wilkinson Jaguar Spares
Park Farm,
Tethering Lane,
Everton,
Nr Doncaster, South Yorks DN10 1XX
Tel: 0777 818061
(New and secondhand spares for all models)

Minters
Blackwell Farm,
Winchendon Rd,
Lower Winchendon,
Aylesbury, Bucks
Tel: 0844 291390
(Various new and secondhand mechanical spares for all models)

G H Nolan
1 St Georges Way,
London SE15
Tel: 01 701 2785
(Spares for all Jaguar models)

Jaguar Spares Specialists
Paxton Mill,
Scaitcliffe Street,
Accrington, Lancs
Tel: 0254 398476
(New and used spares for all models)

Motor Wheel Services
Jeddo Road,
Shepherds Bush,
London W12 9ED
(Wire wheel remanufactures)

A A McInnes
31 Broadgate Crescent,
Almondbury,
Huddersfield, West Yorks
Tel: 0484 35284
(Cylinder head rebuilds for all models)

Three Point Four Jaguar Services
Fitzwilliam Street,
Summer Lane,
Barnsley, South Yorks S70 2NL
Tel: 0226 292601
(Maintenance and restoration of Mark I/II models a speciality)

Ashwater Forge & Foundry
34 Fore Street,
Seaton,
Devon EX12 2AD
Tel: 0297 20787
(Chrome trim remanufactures)

Olaf P. Lund & Son
2-26 Anthony Road,
Saltley, Birmingham B8 3AA
Tel: 021 327 2602
(New and used spares for all models)

F.B. Components
35/41 Edgeway Road,
Marston, Oxford
Tel: 0865 724646
(Full range of new spares for all models)

Norman Motors
100 Mill Lane,
London NW6
Tel: 01 431 0940
(Full range of parts for all models)

P J Langford & Co.
Nottingham
Tel: 0773 713639
(Stainless steel exhausts for all models)

Martin Robey Limited
Pool Road,
Camp Hill Ind. Estate,
Nuneaton, Warks
Tel: 0203 386903
(Remanufactured steel panels for all models, plus wiring harnesses, electrical
items, suspension and steering parts, etc.)

Hyblok Sales Limited
5 Netley Street,
Farnborough, Hants
Tel: 0252 547717
(Nut, bolts, screws and rare items for all models)

Suffolk & Turley
Kelsey Close,
Attleborough Fields Ind. Estate,
Nuneaton, Warks
Tel: 0203 381429
(Leather retrims for all models)

The Vintage & Classic Car Spares Co.
Unit 43,
Hartlebury Trading Estate,
Hartlebury,
Kidderminster, Worcs DY10 4JB
Tel: 0299 251353
(Lights, fittings, switches, electrical items for all models)

Ken Bell
Crooked Timbers,
White Hart Lane,
Guildford, Surrey
Tel: 0483 235153
(Mark II mechanical specialist)

Classic Car Motor Policies Limited
365A Limpsfield Road,
Warlingham,
Surrey CR3 9HA
Tel: 08832 7491/2/3/4
(Classic motor car insurance)

SC Jaguar Components
13 Cobham Way,
Gatwick Road,
Crawley, W. Sussex RH10 2RX
Tel: 0293 547841
(Stainless steel exhaust manufacturers, panel and chrome suppliers)

Classic Dashboards
Bournemouth
Tel: 0202 575167
(Wood veneer refurbishment)

Adam Howell
Tel: 0922 649992
(Chrome trim suppliers)

Ken Jenkins
Unit 4, 2 High Road,
Carlton in Lindrick, Notts
Tel: 0909 732219/730754 or 0836 241101
(New and used spares specialist and Jaguar car sales)

The Sussex Chrome Company
39 Salisbury Road,
Tilgate,
Crawley, West Sussex RH10 5LX
Tel: 0293 551276
(Chrome trim suppliers)

Bridport Jaguar
Unit 2,
Dreadnough Ind. Estate,
Bridport, Dorset DT6 5BU
Tel: 0308 27593
(Spares supply to all models)

Paul Goodyear Investacar Limited
Powmill,
Farnell,
Brechin DD9 6VD
Tel: 067 482 353/4
(Panels, spares, trim and restoration services)

Peter Rees
245 Cyncoed Road,
Cardiff CF2 6NZ
Tel: 0222 751081
(Chromed wire wheel rebuild and supply)

Steven Chennells
Unit 8, Acorn Mews,
Bush Fair,
Harlow, Essex CM18 6NA
Tel: 0279 37081
(Mark I/II spares specialist)

Jaguar Enthusiasts' Club Spares & Specialist Tool Service
c/o Thelma Brotton,
Stoneycroft, Moor Lane,
Birdwell,
Barnsley, South Yorks
Tel: 0226 742829
(Specialist tool and spares remanufacture)

Patrick Lacey Motors
High Road,
Carlton in Lindrick, Notts
(Restoration and refurbishment as well as general maintenance on Jaguar/
Daimler models)

(This is only a partial list. Further details can be obtained from the clubs)